Comptroller of the Currency
Administrator of National Banks

Investment Securities

Comptroller's Handbook
(Section 203)

Narrative and Procedures - March 1990

Assets

Investment Securities
(Section 203)

Table of Contents

Investment Securities
(Section 203)   Introduction

This section discusses money market investments and securities purchased by the bank for its own account. Securities purchased primarily for resale to customers, i.e., trading account securities, are discussed in a separate section of this handbook.

The term "money market" generally refers to the markets for short- term credit instruments, such as commercial paper, bankers' acceptances, negotiable certificates of deposit, repurchase agreements, and federal funds. Although not carried in the investment account, such instruments generally are handled by the investment officer. The highly liquid nature of such investments allows the bank to employ temporarily idle funds in interest bearing assets that usually can be converted quickly into cash. The speed of conversion, however, depends on the quality of the investment. Quality can be monitored through credit analysis, emphasizing a review of current financial information, the use of specializing rating services, and frequent collateral valuation. Since money market transactions generally involve a large volume of funds, deficiencies in credit or administrative policies can quickly result in serious problems. The investment policy should include limitations on authority of personnel, restrictions regarding asset type, and amount and established credit standards. Compliance with policy guidelines should be assured through adequate internal controls, audit coverage, and internal supervisory review.

Investment securities, representing obligations purchased for the bank's own account, may include United States government obligations; various Federal agency bonds; state, county, and municipal issues, special revenue bonds; industrial revenue bonds; and certain corporate debt securities. Securities included in the investment account should provide a reasonable rate of return commensurate with safety, which must take precedence. Investment considerations should come into play only after provision for all cash needs and reasonable loan demands have been met. Accordingly, an investment account should contain some securities that may be quickly converted into cash by immediate sale or by bonds maturing. Hence, liquidity and marketability are of the utmost importance. A bond is a liquid asset if its maturity is short and if there is assurance that it will be paid at maturity. It is marketable if it may be sold quickly at a price commensurate with its yield and quality. The highest quality bonds have those two desirable qualities.

Investments, like loans, are extensions of credit involving risks that carry commensurate rewards. However, risks in the investment portfolio should be minimized to ensure that liquidity and marketability are maintained. Bank management must recognize that the investment account is primarily a secondary reserve for liquidity rather than a vehicle to generate speculative profits. Speculation in marginal securities to generate more favorable yields is an unsound banking practice.

Occasionally, examiners will have difficulty distinguishing between a loan and a security. Loans result from direct negotiations between a borrower and a lender. A bank will refuse to grant a loan unless the borrower agrees to its terms. A security, on the other hand, is usually acquired through a third party, a broker or dealer in securities. Most securities have standardized terms that can be compared to the terms of other market offerings. Because the terms of most loans do not lend themselves to such comparison, the average investor may not accept the terms of the lending arrangement. Thus, an individual loan cannot be regarded as a readily marketable security.

Limitations and Restrictions on National Banks' Holdings

National banks are governed in their security investments by the seventh paragraph of 12 USC 24 and by the investment securities regulation of the Comptroller of the Currency (12 CFR 1). The investment securities regulation defines investment securities; political subdivision; general obligation; and Type I, II, and III securities, and establishes limitations on the bank's investment in those securities. The law, 12 USC 24, requires that for a security to qualify as an investment security, it be marketable and not predominantly speculative.

For its own account, a bank may purchase Type I securities, which are obligations of the U.S. government or its agencies and general obligations of states and political subdivisions (see 12 USC 24(7)), subject to no limitations, other than the exercise of prudent banking judgment. The purchase of Type II and III securities (see 12 CFR 1.3(d) and (e)) is limited to 10 percent of capital and surplus for each obligor when the purchase is based on adequate evidence of the maker's ability to perform. That limitation is reduced to 5 percent of capital and surplus for all obligors in the aggregate where the purchase judgment is predicated on "reliable estimates." The term "reliable estimates" refers to projections of income and debt service requirements or conditional ratings when factual credit information is not available and when the obligor does not have a record of performance. Securities purchased subject to the 5 percent limitation may, in fact, become eligible for the 10 percent limitation once a satisfactory financial record has been established. There are additional limitations on specific securities ruled eligible for investment by the OCC that are detailed in 12 CFR 1.3. The par value, not the book value or purchase price, of the security is the basis for computing the limitations. However, the limitations do not apply to securities acquired through debts previously contracted.

When a bank purchases an investment security that is convertible into stock or has stock purchase warrants attached, entries must be made by the bank at the time of the purchase to write down the cost of the security to an amount representing the investment value of the security exclusive of the conversion feature or the attached stock purchase warrants. The purchase of securities convertible into stock at the option of the issuer is prohibited (12 CFR 1.10).

Mortgage Backed Securities

Most mortgage backed securities (MBS) pass-through obligations are issued by or obligations of GNMA, FNMA, or FHLMC. Accordingly, banks may invest in them in unlimited amounts.

The Secondary Mortgage Market Enhancement Act of 1984 (SMMEA) amended 12 USC 24(7) and allows national banks to purchase and hold "mortgage related securities" without any statutory limitation. Collateralized Mortgage Obligations (CMO's) and Real Estate Mortgage Investment Conduits (REMIC's) are "mortgage related securities" for the purposes of SMMEA if they are offered and sold pursuant to Section 4 (5) of the Securities Act of 1933 (15 USC 77d(5)); or are mortgage related securities as that term is defined in Section 3(a) (41) of the Securities Exchange Act of 1934 (15 USC 78c(a) (41)).

Information as to when a "mortgage related security" is covered by SMMEA is usually found in the security's prospectus or offering circular. Look in the index of the prospectus under SMMEA or legal matters. A privately issued MBS that is not fully collateralized by U.S. government or Federal agency obligations must be supported by a credible opinion that it is covered by SMMEA. In the absence of such an opinion, this type of security may be subject to a Type III investment limit or, depending upon the facts, considered ineligible for national bank investment. Interest Only (IOs) portions and Residual interests in any of the above listed securities are not unconditional obligations of the issuer, and, accordingly, these derivative products are not eligible for the same holding limitations.

Private Placements

The absence of a public market for securities which are "privately placed" makes them ineligible as investments for national bank investment portfolios. Refer to handbook section 411 for a more complete discussion of private placements.

Mutual Funds and Investment Companies

A national bank may purchase for its own account without limitation shares of investment companies as long as the portfolios of such companies consist solely of obligations that are eligible for purchase without limitation by national banks for their own account pursuant to the provisions of paragraph Seventh of 12 USC 24. Shares of investment companies whose portfolios contain investments subject to the limits of 12 USC 24 or 84 may only be held in an amount not to exceed 10 percent of capital and surplus. That is, a bank may invest only an amount not to exceed 10 percent of its capital and surplus in each such investment company. Also, to be eligible for national bank investment, the investment company must be registered with the Securities and Exchange Commission under the Investment Company Act of 1940 and Securities Act of 1933 or be a privately offered fund sponsored by an affiliated commercial bank. This can be determined by a review of the fund's prospectus.

Banks that invest in such investment companies must be aware of the possibility that a bank may violate the 10 percent limitation because of the cumulative holdings of a particular security in the portfolios of more than one investment company or in combination with the bank's direct holdings. Accordingly, a bank that has invested in shares of more than one investment company must determine that its pro rata share of any security in the fund portfolio subject to the 10 percent limitation does not exceed it by being combined with the bank's pro rata share of that security held by all other funds in which the bank has invested and with the Bank's own direct investment portfolio holdings. Therefore, the holdings of investment companies whose shares are held by the bank must be reviewed quarterly.

The bank's investment policy as formally approved by its board of directors should: (1) provide specifically for such investments; (2) require that for initial investments in specific investment companies prior approval of the board of directors be obtained and recorded in the official board minutes; and (3) ensure that procedures, standards, and controls for managing such investments are implemented prior to making the investment.

A bank's investment in shares of investment companies that use futures, forward placement and options contracts, repurchase agreements, and securities lending arrangements as part of their portfolio management strategies is permitted, provided that those instruments would be considered acceptable for use in a national bank's own investment portfolio.

In addition to considering the types of instruments used for each investment company and applicable investment limits, national bank portfolio managers should weigh the practical liquidity of holdings of investment company shares. Mutual Funds Shares and Unit Investment Trust (UIT) units are much less marketable generally than many types of "investment securities," particularly U.S. government and federal agency issues. Indeed, certain investment company fee structures, such as "deferred contingency" fees (declining rear-end load fees), may actually impede marketability. Most municipal authorities will not accept mutual fund shares as collateral for pledge against uninsured public deposits or for other pledging purposes. Units of closed-end tax exempt UITs may present particular liquidity problems because they may not be readily redeemable nor have a secondary market.

Generally Accepted Accounting Principles and the instructions for the quarterly Reports of Condition require that bank holdings of investment company shares be reported at the lower of the aggregate cost or market value. The market value of "open-end" investment company shares reported should be based on net asset value rather than offering price; shares in "closed-end" investment companies should be marked to the bid price. In no case should the carrying value of investment company holdings be increased above their aggregate cost as a result of net unrealized gains. Net unrealized losses on marketable equity securities and subsequent recoveries of those losses should be excluded from the income statement and be reported instead (reduced by the applicable income tax effect) as an adjustment to "Undivided Profits and Capital Reserves." A loss other than a temporary one on an individual investment held by the fund should be changed to noninterest expense on the income statement.

As part of the market value determination, mutual funds sales fees, both "front-end load" and "deferred contingency," must be deducted to reflect more accurately the current value of fund shares. Consequently, unless the market value of such shares increases sufficiently to offset those fees, their amount must be reflected at the end of the first reporting period as unrealized losses and charged against "Undivided Profits and Capital Reserves."

Generally, banks are prohibited from investing in stocks. However, detailed below are a number of exceptions to that rule:

Permitted Stock Holdings by National Banks

Type of stock	Authorizing statute and limitation
Federal Reserve Bank	12 USC 282—Subscription must equal 6 percent of the bank's capital and surplus, 3 percent paid in. (Regulation I, Federal Reserve Board; 12 CFR 209)
Safe deposit corporation	12 USC 24—15 percent of capital and surplus.
Corporation holding bank premises	12 USC 371(d)—100 percent of capital. Limitation includes total direct and indirect investment in bank premises in any form. Maximum limitation may be exceeded with permission of the District Deputy Comptroller (12 CFR 7.3100).
Small business investment company	15 USC 682(b)—5 percent of capital and surplus. After January 10, 1968, national banks are prohibited from acquiring shares of such a corporation if, upon making the acquisition: • The aggregate amount of shares in small business investment companies then held by the bank would exceed 5 percent of its capital and surplus.
Banking service corporation	12 USC 1861 and 1862—10 percent of capital and surplus. Limitation includes total direct and indirect investment in any form. Also, corporation must be owned by one or more banks.
Foreign banking corporation	12 USC 601 and 618—10 percent of capital and surplus with the provision that capital and surplus must be $1 million or more.
Corporation authorized under Title IX of the Housing and Urban Development Act of 1968 (amendments not included)	12 USC 1718(f)—No limit.
Federal National Mortgage Association	12 USC 1718(f)—No limit.
Bank's own stock	12 USC 83—Shares of the bank's own stock may not be acquired or taken as security for loans, except as necessary to prevent loss from a debt previously contracted in good faith. Stock, so acquired, must be disposed of within 6 months of

Type of stock	Authorizing statute and limitation
	the date of acquisition.
Corporate Stock acquired through debts previously contracted (DPC) transaction.	Case law has established that stock of any corporation may be acquired to prevent loss from a debt previously contracted in good faith. However, if the stock is not disposed of within a reasonable time period, it loses its status as a DPC transaction and becomes a prohibited holding under 12 USC 24(7). The maximum time such stock can be retained generally is regarded to be 5 years. The maximum time limit for stock of affiliates acquired through a DPC transaction, and not held within the limitations of specific statutes, is 2 years.
Corporate stock acquired as a dividend from a small business investment company (SBIC)	12 CFR 7.7535—No limit. Stock of any corporation may be acquired and retained, if received as a dividend on SBIC stock.
Operating subsidiaries	12 CFR 7.10—No limit. Stock of any operating subsidiary corporation, the functions or activities of which are limited to those authorized to a national bank, may be acquired and held without limitation, provided that at least 80 percent of the voting stock of the subsidiary is owned by the bank. The establishment of an operating subsidiary requires the prior approval of the OCC (12 CFR 7.7378 through 7.7380).
State Housing Corporation incorporated in the state in which the association is located	12 USC 24—5 percent of its capital stock, paid in and unimpaired plus 5 percent of its unimpaired surplus fund when considered together with loans and commitments made to the corporation.
Agricultural Credit Corporation	12 USC 24—20 percent of capital and surplus unless the association owns over 80 percent. No limit if association owns 80 percent or more.
Government National Mortgage Association	12 USC 24—No limit.
Student Loan Marketing Association	12 USC 24—No limit.
Minibank Capital Corporation	12 CFR 7.7480—2 percent of capital and surplus. Aggregate investment in all such projects should not exceed 5 percent of capital and surplus.
Charitable foundations	12 CFR 7.7445—Contribution in any one year not to exceed income tax deduction.
Community development corporation	12 CFR 7.7480—2 percent of capital and surplus. Aggregate investments in such projects should not exceed 5 percent of capital and surplus
Bankers' banks	12 USC 24—10 percent of capital stock and paid in and unimpaired surplus. Bankers' bank must be insured by the FDIC, owned exclusively by other banks, and engaged solely in providing banking services to other banks and their officers, directors, or employees. Ownership shall not result in any bank acquiring more than 5 percent of any class of voting securities of the bankers' bank.

Investment Policy

As provided in 12 USC 24(7), a bank's board of directors is responsible for supervising the bank's activities. Well-managed banks should have written policies that provide guidelines for the investment officer, investment committee, and those dealing in securities.

The basic objectives of a sound investment policy are the same for all banks, but the emphasis placed on each objective will vary according to the individual bank's needs. The basic objectives include:

- Minimizing risks.
- Generating a favorable return on investments without undue compromise of the other objectives.
- Providing for adequate liquidity.
- Meeting pledging requirements.

To insure that the directors do not delegate policy decisions, the investment policy must encompass more than a philosophical description of objectives.

The investment policy should include guidelines on the quality and quantity of each type of security to be held, with the stipulation that securities acquired will be eligible and in amounts conforming to the limitations prescribed by 12 USC 24(7) and 23 CFR 1. Credit quality is of major importance. United States government obligations are the highest quality credits and are the most readily marketable. Therefore, an adequate amount of such securities should be in the portfolio. They are "riskless" from a credit standpoint but are subject to price fluctuations because of changes in money market interest rates. Of course, long-term issues tend to fluctuate more widely than the shorter term ones.

Federal agency securities are the next highest in quality. For securities with identical maturities, the yield spread averages between 10 and 20 basis points above U.S. government bonds. Similar investments that currently enjoy wide acceptance in the banking community are U.S. government guaranteed public housing authority issues. New housing authority and public housing authority notes or bonds provide the investor with tax exempt income and a full faith and credit guaranty of the U.S. government.

Other tax exempt bonds enjoy varying levels of indirect U.S. government support. "Pre-refunded" or "escrowed" bonds are often fully and directly secured by obligations issued by or otherwise supported by the full faith and credit of the United States. Certain municipal housing bonds are partially payable from rental subsidies and/or mortgage credit insurance provided by federal agencies. Pools of partially guaranteed student loans are sometimes pledged for payment of municipal higher education bonds. There are numerous programs that provide federal backing for municipal bonds. Care must be taken to distinguish between those issues that are federally guaranteed and those that are not.

High quality municipal bonds frequently are desirable because of their tax exempt status. Many municipal bonds, however, possess an unfavorable market aspect. Except for high quality issues of larger municipalities, municipals often are not readily marketable or may produce sizeable spreads between bid and ask prices. The spread may be so wide it may cost the selling bank a sizeable portion of a year's interest. Most banks hold local securities as a service to their community. The aggregate of such holdings should be reasonable relative to the capital structure of the bank.

Monthly rating service publications are useful in determining the investment quality of municipal and corporate obligations. The standard bond rating symbols are indicated in the order of their credit quality.

Standard & Poor's	Moody's	Description
Bank Quality Investments		
AAA	Aaa	Highest grade obligations.
AA	Aa	High grade obligations.
A	A-1, A	Upper medium grade.
BBB	Baa-1,Baa	Medium grade, on the borderline between definitely sound obligations and those containing predominantly speculative elements. Generally, the lowest quality bond that may qualify for bank investment.
Speculative and Defaulted Issues		
BB	Ba	Lower medium grade with only minor investment characteristics.
B	B	Low grade, default probable.

D	Ca, c	Lowest rated class, defaulted, extremely poor prospects.
	Provisional or Conditional Rating	
Rating-P	Con. (Rating)	Debt service requirements are largely dependent on reliable estimates as to future events.

A program for obtaining and evaluating current information on securities in the investment portfolio should be an integral part of a bank's investment policy. At minimum, the examiner should expect such a program to include credit reviews prior to purchase and credit updates on all non-rated issues, municipal obligations with a credit rating that has declined, special revenue and other debt obligations with limited or no marketability, speculative and defaulted issues, and stocks acquired through DCP transactions. Credit analysis is necessary to determine if an investment is eligible for the bank to own. The directors' failure to exercise that responsibility can result in violations of law and potential personal liability.

General obligations of state and municipal issuers are exempt from the restrictive provisions of 12 USC 24 and 12 CFR 1. However, a bank must exercise prudent banking judgment in managing the general obligation section of its portfolio.

The investment policy should require evaluation of the following minimum credit information before a bank acquires general obligation municipal bonds.

- Debt burden of municipality:
  - Relationship of debt burden to property valuation.
  - Reasonableness of debt burden on a per capita basis.
  - Sinking fund provisions.
  - Historical trends of debt.
  - Future debt service requirements.

- Tax burden of municipality:
  - Assessed valuation, including basis of assessment.
  - Relationship of tax burden to property valuation.
  - Tax collection record.
  - Recent trends in tax rates.

- Quality of budgets:
  - Requirement for balanced budget.
  - Recent trends in budget deficits or surpluses.
  - Cash flow requirements.
  - Accuracy of past estimates of revenues and expenses.
  - Accounting policies.

- Character of community:
  - Economic background.
  - Debt paying ability.
  - Population trends.

Special revenue obligations may have a place in the investment portfolio. They generally are supported solely by service charges established by the issuing governmental authority that owns or operates a facility, such as toll roads, industrial plants, or airports. Because such bonds are not supported by the taxing authority, they generally cannot be regarded as possessing as high a credit quality as general obligations. Special revenue obligations possess many of the characteristics of term loans. Accordingly, a bank should obtain and evaluate appropriate credit information. Factors peculiar to special revenue issues that must be considered separately include:

- The number of times gross revenues covers debt service (coverage).
- The segregation of revenue funds from general funds.
- The flow of revenues to specific reserve accounts.
- Special covenants that may limit default remedies.

The investment policy also should include a maturity program. Each bank should tailor its maturity program to its individual needs, particularly its liquidity requirements. Anticipated loan increases, deposit decreases, and a reserve to meet unexpected liquidity demands should be provided. Accordingly, a reasonable percentage of liabilities should be funded in short-term, high quality investments or money market instruments. Such practices generally will assure a short-term flow of funds that may be reinvested or held to meet liquidity needs. It also is advisable that a maximum allowable maturity be defined in the policy. Investments with unusually long terms are vulnerable to market swings that may depress both their price and their useful liquidity. As a general rule, outstanding maturities should be spaced evenly with the preponderance in short- and medium-term issues.

Concentrations

Policy guidelines for risk diversification should be formulated by bank management in conformance with legal limits and prudent investment practices. Supervisory concern about a bank's investment portfolio diversification should focus on credit risk, interest-rate risk, and market risk associated with concentrations in holdings. Concentrations, or the lack of risk diversification, can result from:

- Single or related issuers.
- Lack of geographic distribution.
- Holdings of obligations with similar characteristics, such as mortgage backed bonds, zero coupon bonds, hospital bonds, etc.
- Holdings of bonds having the same trustee.
- Holdings of bonds having the same credit enhancer, such as insurer or letter of credit issuer.
- Holdings of securitized loans having the same originator, packager, or guarantor.
- Similar credit ratings, particularly in low ratings.

Concentrations of risk arising from both a bank's portfolio of securities and loans may be compatible with a bank's management strategy. However, having securities and loans repayable from the same general source, or with common originators, enhancers, or servicers greatly increases the bank's vulnerability to unforeseen credit and liquidity risks. Bank risk managers need to be aware of and monitor these types of bank-wide risk concentrations. They need to develop prudent concentration limits and institute name and type limitations for securities and loans. Bank managers which do not monitor concentration risks and consider the potential for concentrations in the bank's invested funds and loan portfolios are increasing the risk to bank capital and are remiss in carrying out their responsibilities.

The investment policy should take into consideration the applicable Federal and state income tax laws and the individual bank's tax position. Finally, the investment portfolio should be reviewed at least annually by the board of directors and quarterly by senior officers of the bank. Sufficient analytical data must be provided to allow the board and senior management to make an informed judgment of the investment policy's effectiveness. Such reviews should consider the information discussed in this section as well as the current market value of the portfolio.

The responsibility for supervising the bank's investment account rests solely with the board of directors and cannot be delegated to a correspondent bank, an advisory service, a brokerage house, or a rating service.

Selection of Securities Dealers

It is common for bank investment portfolio managers to rely on the advice of securities sales representatives for recommendation of proposed investments, investment strategies, and the timing and pricing of securities transactions. Accordingly, it is important for bank management to know the securities firms and the personnel with whom they deal. An investment portfolio manager should not engage in securities transactions with any securities dealer that is unwilling to provide complete and timely disclosure of its financial condition. Management must review the dealer's financial statements and make an informed judgment about the ability of the dealer to honor its commitments. An inquiry into the general reputation of the dealer also is necessary.

The board of directors and/or an appropriate board committee should review and approve a list of securities firms with whom the bank is authorized to do business. The dealer selection process should include:

- Consideration of the ability of the securities dealer and its subsidiaries or affiliates to fulfill commitments as evidenced by capital strength and operating results disclosed in current financial data, annual reports, credit reports, etc.

- Inquiry into the dealer's general reputation for financial stability and fair and honest dealings with customers, including past or current financial institution customers of the securities dealer.

- Contact with appropriate state or federal securities regulators and securities industry self-regulatory organizations, such as the National Association of Securities Dealers, concerning any formal enforcement actions against the dealer or its affiliates or associated personnel.

- Inquiry, as appropriate, into the background of the sales representative to determine his or her experience and expertise.

- Determination of whether the bank has appropriate procedures to establish possession or control of securities purchased. Purchased securities and repurchase agreement collateral should be kept in safekeeping with selling dealers only when (1) the board is completely satisfied as to the creditworthiness of the securities dealer; and (2) the aggregate value securities held in safekeeping in this manner is within credit limitations that have been approved by the board of directors, or a committee of the board, for unsecured transactions.

As a part of the process of managing a bank's relationships with securities dealers, the board of directors may also want to consider prohibiting those employees, who are directly involved in purchasing and selling securities for the bank, from engaging in personal securities transactions with the same securities firm the bank uses for its transactions without specific board approval and periodic review. Such prohibition could be included in the bank's code of ethics or code of conduct. The board also may want to adopt a policy applicable to directors, officers, or employees concerning receipt of gifts, gratuities, or travel expenses from approved dealer firms and their personnel (also see the Bank Bribery Law, 18 USC 215 and interpretive releases).

Delegation of Portfolio Discretion

Bank managers sometimes delegate investment decision making authority to individuals who are not bank or affiliate employees. This might be done based upon the promise of substantially increased return on a bank's securities because of a portfolio advisor or consultant's ability: to act quickly on buy or sell opportunities and to execute transactions at the best possible price; to aggressively use market data and their knowledge of new securities instruments; to advantageously time the transaction execution; select the securities dealer used; and, search for and negotiate prices predicated on volume discounts.

The responsibility for supervising a national bank's investment portfolio rests solely with the board of directors. The directors of a national bank have a fiduciary duty to the shareholders, depositors, and creditors of the bank, and are charged with an implied trust to use bank funds only for permitted purposes. The OCC has stated in Interpretive Ruling number 7.4425 and has informed bank directors (see chapter III The Director's Book—The Role of a National Bank Director and section 501 Comptroller's Handbook for National

Bank Examiners) that directors cannot delegate responsibility for their duties, but can only assign the authority for performance of those duties to others. The OCC does not object to delegation of authority to perform securities transactions to individuals not employed by the bank, or to unaffiliated firms, provided that supervision of those delegated is at the same level the OCC expects of bank employees with such authority.

When a bank's board of directors assigns authority to take investment action (i.e., make buy or sell determinations) to non-employees or to nonaffiliated companies, it effectively removes portfolio control from the bank management. Accordingly, such investments no longer meet the requirements of Generally Accepted Accounting Principals (GAAP) for securities portfolio accounting, and securities transactions must be recorded and reported on an independently established mark to market, or lower of cost or market basis.

Open Contractual Commitments to Purchase or Sell Securities

When Issued

The most common type of open contractual commitment to purchase or sell securities encountered by examiners is a "when issued" or "when and if issued" security transaction (WI). WI securities are new issue securities that have been awarded to a buyer but have not yet been paid for or delivered. A WI period may last several weeks or more than a month. WI periods for U.S. government securities are shorter than those for federal agency or municipal securities. During the WI period, the buyer may pay a small deposit on U.S. government transactions but usually pays nothing on federal agency and municipal trades while retaining all ownership rights to the underlying security. WI securities enjoying wide market distribution will usually begin to trade in the secondary market during the WI period, and a bank may sell its rights to the security prior to paying for it. Owning rights to a security and being able to sell those rights before paying for them has certain leverage implications that may be incompatible with prudent banking or investment practice.

Outstanding WI commitments to purchase securities should be reviewed and priced to determine their impact on liquidity, earnings, and risk diversification. Purchases and sales of WI securities between examinations should be reviewed to determine if the volume of transactions is consistent with investment policy objectives. Transactions between examinations should also be inspected to determine if WI speculation has resulted in the sale of profitable WI positions, while nonprofitable WI purchases are retained and recorded in the investment portfolio at a carrying value equivalent to the original cost of the security. If the investment portfolio is being used to "backstop" WI speculation, the book value of the retained securities should be adjusted to reflect the unrealized loss as of settlement date.

Forward Placement Contracts

Another common type of open contractual commitment to purchase securities is a forward placement transaction. Forward placements are purchases or sales of securities at fixed prices for mandatory, but delayed, delivery on a future date. Contractual commitments to purchase or sell securities on a forward placement basis do not involve cash deposits or margins. Forward placement contract maturities run from 30 days to several years. Contract prices reflect investors' interest rate expectations.

Forward contracts are cash market transactions, other than "when issued" transactions, that specify delivery (settlement) in excess of thirty (30) days following the trade date. They are neither traded on organized exchanges nor are their terms standardized. Forward contracts can only be terminated by agreement of both parties to the transaction.

Forward placement contracts are usually associated with the origination and issuance of mortgage-backed securities. A mortgage banker wishing to hedge the risk of loss resulting from interest rate fluctuations often agrees to forward sell an anticipated, but as yet unissued, security at a price assuring a profit. Investors having predictable funds flows may wish to acquire rights to a security to be delivered at a fixed price and yield on a future date.

Examiners should review outstanding forward placement commitments to determine the impact of completion of forward placement transactions on liquidity and earnings. The volume and nature of transactions should be consistent with investment policy objectives. Recordkeeping and management reporting systems should facilitate ready review and control of forward placement trade positions and maturities. Losses on delivered securities should be tested and any unrecorded losses booked immediately upon discovery.

Standby Contracts

Standby contracts are optional delivery forward placement contracts. The buyer of a standby contract (put option) pays a fee for the right or option to sell (deliver) an agreed upon amount of specified securities to the issuer of the standby contract at a specified price and at a specified future date.

Financial Futures Contracts

Financial futures contracts are commodities contracts and are similar to forward placement contracts in that they involve the purchase or sale of a security or money market instrument at a fixed price and yield for delivery at a future date. Futures contracts differ from forward placement contracts because they are traded on an organized exchange that guarantees performance according to contract terms. The exchange also requires customers to pay initial and continuous maintenance margin.

Purchasers and sellers of futures contracts must pay a small initial margin deposit at the time a contract is entered into. The deposit must be maintained at a minimum level. When net unrealized losses on contracts exceed that minimum deposit, the bank must pay over maintenance margin sufficient to bring the deposit level to an acceptable minimum amount. Conversely, if the market value of the contract increases, net unrealized gains are deposited to the bank's margin account.

Maintenance margin in excess of minimum requirements may be withdrawn or used as margin deposit on additional transactions. Margin calculations and, if necessary, margin calls are made daily. Statements of account (margin runs) are rendered weekly.

Margin requirements may be satisfied by deposits of cash, U.S. government securities, or stand-by letters of credit. Unrealized loss or gain should generally be reflected in the bank's profit and loss statement as maintenance margin accounts are adjusted.

Interest rate futures contracts are entered into to speculate on interest rate movement or to hedge the risk of losses resulting from interest rate fluctuations. OCC has adopted a policy of discouraging speculative use of interest rate futures. Unfortunately, there is no clear distinction between a hedger and a speculator; the terms are not always mutually exclusive.

Financial futures and forward placement contracts are not considered investment securities within the meaning of 12 USC 24(7). However, with the following distinctions, the use of these contracts is considered to be an activity incidental to banking. The minimal guidelines for national banks that engage in these markets are also described.

Distinctions

For investment portfolio or non-dealer operations in fixed rate assets, banks should evaluate the interest rate risk exposure resulting from their overall investment activities to insure that the positions they take in futures, forwards, and standby contracts markets will reduce that exposure. Short positions in futures and forwards contracts should relate reasonably to existing or anticipated cash positions and should be used to enhance liquidity of the portfolio. As asset yields are upgraded, contract gains should be used to offset losses resulting from the sale of portfolio securities rather than using short hedges against portfolio holdings for income generation. Long positions in futures and forwards should reasonably reflect the bank's investment strategy and ability to fulfill its commitments.

Asset-liability management involves the matching of fixed rate and interest-sensitive assets and liabilities to maintain liquidity and profitability. Futures and forwards contracts may be used as a general hedge against the interest rate exposure associated with undesired mismatches in interest-sensitive assets and liabilities. Long positions in contracts could be used as a hedge against funding interest-sensitive assets with fixed-rate sources of funds. Short positions in contracts could be used as a hedge against funding fixed-rate assets with interest-sensitive liabilities.

Dealer-bank trading activities that employ futures, forwards, and standby contracts should be performed in accordance with safe and sound banking practices related reasonably to the bank's legally permitted trading activities.

Minimal Guidelines

The board of directors should consider any plan to engage in those activities and should endorse specific written policies in authorizing them. Policy objectives must outline permissible contract strategies and their relationships to other banking activities. Recordkeeping systems must be sufficiently detailed to permit internal auditors and examiners to determine whether operating personnel have acted according to authorized objectives. Bank personnel are expected to describe and document in detail how the positions they have taken in futures, forwards, and standby contracts contribute to attaining the bank's objectives.

The board of directors should establish limits applicable to futures, forward, and standby contract positions. The board, a duly authorized board committee, or the bank's internal auditors should review periodically (at least monthly) contract positions to ascertain conformance with such limits.

The bank should maintain general ledger memorandum accounts or commitment registers to identify adequately and control all commitments to make or take delivery of securities. Such registers and supporting journals should, at a minimum, include:

- The type and amount of each contract.
- The maturity date of each contract.
- The current market price and cost of each contract.
- The amount of money held in margin accounts.

All open positions should be reviewed and market values determined at least monthly (or more often depending on the volume and magnitude of positions), regardless of whether the bank is required to deposit margins for a given contract. Underlying security commitments relating to open futures and forwards contracts should not be reported on the balance sheet. Margin deposits and any unrealized losses (and, in certain instances, unrealized gains) are usually the only entries to be recorded on the books. All futures and forwards contracts should be valued on the basis of either market or the lower of cost or market, at the option of the bank. Forward contracts executed for trading account purposes should be valued on a basis consistent with other trading positions. Losses on standby contracts must be computed only by the issuer (the party committed to purchase under the contract) and only when the market value of the security is below the contract price, reduced by the amount of the deferred fee income. Market basis for forward and standby contracts should be based on the market value of the underlying security, except where publicly quoted forward prices are available. All losses resulting from monthly contract value determinations should be recognized as a current expense item. Those banks that value contracts on a market basis will recognize gains as a current income item.

Fees received by a bank for the issuance of a standby contract should be deferred at initiation of the contract and accounted for as follows:

- Upon expiration of an unexercised contract, as income.
- Upon a negotiated settlement of the contract prior to maturity, as an adjustment to the expense of such settlement, and the net should be transferred to the income account.
- Upon exercise of the contract, as an adjustment to the basis of the acquired securities. Such adjusted cost basis should be compared to market value of those securities.

Bank financial reports should disclose in an explanatory note any futures, forwards, and standby contract activity that materially affects the bank's financial condition. To minimize their credit risk, banks should implement a system for monitoring exposure associated with various customers and dealers with whom operating personnel are authorized to transact business. Banks should establish other internal controls, including periodic reports to management and internal audit programs, to assure adherence to bank policy, and to prevent unauthorized trading and other abuses.

Long-term contracts over 150 days, which give the other party to the contract the option to deliver securities to the bank, ordinarily should not be issued. Regulatory authorities have found that often such contracts are related not to the investment or business needs of the institution, but primarily to the earning of fee income or to speculating on future interest rate movements.

National banks wishing to engage in the futures, forwards, and standby contracts markets must submit a letter notice stating their intention to the Deputy Comptroller for their district.

Banks should enter into interest rate futures contracts primarily to reduce the risk of loss from interest rate fluctuations and not to produce income.

A simple use of interest rate futures by a bank would involve a direct offset or hedge to a particular investment or portion of its investment portfolio. For example, a banker wishing to limit the effects of portfolio depreciation could purchase a futures contract(s) to deliver securities (short). If interest rates rise and bond prices decline, profits on the futures contract can be used to offset the increase in unrealized loss in portfolio. Depreciated securities could then be sold at a loss without impairing current earnings. The sale proceeds could be reinvested at higher yields to insure improved future earnings. Failure to sell the depreciated securities would have the effect of improving current earnings at the expense of future earnings. If, however, interest rates decline, the short futures contract would be reversed at a loss. This current loss could be offset by the sale of portfolio investments at a gain. However, sale proceeds would have to be reinvested at lower prevailing yields, thus impairing future earnings. Examiners reviewing futures transactions must be aware of the earnings trade-offs inherent in many futures transactions. Anxiety for short-term income should not be allowed to impair future earnings prospects or to erode the practical liquidity of portfolios.

Interest rate futures contracts may also be used to reduce the negative impact of interest rate fluctuations on funds management strategies. Take the example of a banker who anticipates rising interest rates. He or she may attempt to increase the bank's ratio of variable rate assets versus variable rate liabilities and to lock-in fixed rate source funds at current rates. That would probably be done by extending liability maturities and simultaneously shortening maturities on fixed rate earning assets. Thus, the banker would hope that the spread between interest earned and paid will widen as rates rise. Interest rate futures can then be used to limit the level of interest rate risk associated with the funds management commitment by buying a futures contract to take delivery of securities (long). If, contrary to expectations, the general level of interest rates goes down, the futures contract can be sold at a profit. The profit may be used to offset losses by making the wrong funds management commitment. Futures transactions, employed as part of a funds management strategy, should be reviewed to determine if a reasonable correlation exists between the type, amount, and maturity of the futures instrument(s) and the bank's strategy and interest rate expectations.

Examiners must be satisfied that policies and internal control systems will prevent unauthorized trading and that losses are recognized as they are incurred.

Investment policy should provide for position limits for all types of open contractual commitments to purchase or sell securities. Limits should be considered in aggregate, by type and nature (long and short), by maturity month, by open or gapped position. There should be a logical relationship between investment policy limits on the amount of the securities underlying WI, forwards and futures contracts, and the position limit per type of contract;

i.e., if investment policy guidelines limit the holding of 30-year maturity federal agency securities to a certain amount, that limit should include all WI, forward, or futures contract positions in similar securities.

Position limits for forward placements must also consider the credit risk associated with a dealer on the other side of a trade being able to perform according to contract terms. Position limits per dealer based on credit determinations are appropriate for forward placement commitments.

Investment policies must explain the manner and frequency of position valuations because of the leverage associated with open contractual commitments to purchase or sell securities. The desired frequency of pricing is associated with the volume and nature of activities; monthly pricings are the minimally acceptable frequency. Pricing should be obtained from sources independent of the dealer on the other side of a trade. If bank management cannot obtain regular independent price quotes, they should stop making open contractual commitments to buy or sell securities.

Investment policies must also include a "stop loss" sale or consultation provision that relates to a predetermined loss exposure limit. If losses in open contractual commitment positions reach a certain unacceptable level, the position would be automatically sold out or consultation would ensue in order to rethink investment strategies. This "stop loss" exposure limit should have a reasonable correlation to the bank's capital structure and earnings trends as well as the overall levels of risk inherent in other types of banking activity.

Investment policies should also formalize personnel responsibilities in open contractual commitment areas. Purchase and sale authorizations should be fixed. Transactions should require prior dual authorization.

Open contractual commitment internal control procedures should be reviewed to determine if one person can assume an unwarranted degree of control over the nature and extent of WI, futures, and forward placement commitments. Recordkeeping systems must record transactions on a trade date basis. General ledger memorandum accounts and supporting records must be maintained. Posting to those accounts should be originated and reviewed by persons who do not also have the authority to execute transactions. Ledgers should be periodically compared to broker confirmations and/or account statements. Reports to senior management and the directorate should present enough information to allow them to make an informed judgment as to the prudence of the activities.

Customer Securities Transactions

"Recordkeeping and Confirmation Requirements for Securities Transactions," 12 CFR 12, applies to every national bank that effects securities transactions, including discount brokerage activities, for customers. The regulation establishes requirements for maintaining records, notifying customers, and setting forth specific written policies. Transactions that are subject to the rules of the Municipal Securities Rulemaking Board are not subject to 12 CFR 12.

Unsuitable Investment Portfolio Practices

Trading

The terms "trading" or "overtrading" refer to excessive turnover in the bank's investment portfolio which is not consistent with the bank's stated investment objectives or legitimate needs. Investment securities may be carried in the bank's investment portfolio at amortized cost only when the bank can demonstrate the intent and ability to hold the securities to their maturity. When securities transactions are entered into in anticipation of short-term gains, they are no longer characteristic of investment portfolio activities and should be conducted in a securities trading account and periodically marked to their market value.

Securities trading should only take place in a closely supervised trading account and be undertaken only by institutions that have strong capital and current earnings positions.

Trading in the investment portfolio is characterized by a high volume of purchase and sale activity, which when considered in light of a short holding period, clearly demonstrates management's intent to profit from short-term price movements. Trading in a bank's securities portfolio should be criticized, and the board of directors should be advised to discontinue the practice. It is an unsafe and unsound practice to record and report securities holdings that result from trading transactions using accounting standards intended for investment portfolio transactions. The discipline associated with accounting standards applicable to trading accounts is necessary. Securities held in trading accounts should be periodically (at least monthly) marked to market, with unrealized gain or losses recognized in current income. Prices used in the periodic evaluations should be obtained from sources independent of the securities dealer from whom the securities were purchased or to whom the securities were sold. Securities fraud may be charged if the reporting of trading activities as investment portfolio activities results in an intentionally misleading published financial report for a publicly traded company.

"When Issued" Securities Trading

"When issued" securities trading is the buying and selling of securities in the interim between the announcement of an offering and the issuance and payment date of the securities. A purchaser of a "when issued" security acquires all the risks and rewards of owning a security and may sell the "when issued" security at a profit before taking delivery and paying for it. Frequent purchase and sale of securities during the "when issued" period generally indicate trading activity and should not be conducted in a bank's investment portfolio.

"Pair-offs"

A "pair-off" is a security purchase transaction that is closed out or sold at, or prior to, the settlement date. For example, an investment portfolio manager will commit to purchase a security. Then, prior to the predetermined settlement date, the portfolio manager will "pair-off" the purchase with a sale of the same security prior to, or on, the original settlement date. Profits or losses on the transaction are settled by one party to the transaction remitting to the counter party the difference between the purchase and sale price. Like "when issued" trading, "pair-offs" permit speculation on price movements without paying for the securities.

Corporate or Extended Settlement

Regular-way settlement for transactions in U.S. government and federal agency securities is one business day after the trade date. Regular-way settlement for corporate and municipal securities is five business days after the trade date. The use of a corporate settlement method (5 business days) or extended settlement (6 to 30 days) for U.S. government securities purchases appears to be offered by dealers to facilitate speculation similar to "pair-offs" and "when issued" trading.

Short Sales

A short sale is the sale of a security that is not owned. The purpose of a short sale is generally to speculate on the fall in the price of the security. Short sales are speculative transactions that should be conducted in a trading account, and when conducted in the investment portfolio, they are considered to be unsuitable.

Gains Trading

"Gains trading" is a securities trading activity conducted in an investment portfolio, and is often termed "active portfolio management." "Gains trading" is characterized by the purchase of a security as an investment, and the subsequent sale of that same security at a profit within several days, weeks, or months. Those securities initially purchased with the intent to resell are retained as investment portfolio assets if they cannot be sold at a profit. These "losers" are retained in the investment portfolio because investment portfolio holdings are accounted for at cost, and losses are not recognized unless the security is sold. "Gains trading" often results in a portfolio of securities with extended maturities, lower credit quality, high market depreciation, and limited practical liquidity.

In many cases, "gains trading" has involved the trading of "when issued" securities, "pair-offs," or "corporate settlements" because the extended settlement period associated with these practices allows speculators the opportunity for substantial price changes to occur before payment for the securities is due. It has also involved the use of dealer supplied repurchase agreement financing to carry securities holdings.

In other cases, management accumulates securities positions and just waits for the right market conditions to sell and take gains. A repetitive pattern of sales and gains taken during attractive markets, and no sales during adverse markets, suggests that securities are being held for resale, and they should be marked to the lower of cost or market.

Coupon Stripping

Coupon stripping involves detaching unmatured coupons from securities and selling either the coupons or the remaining, mutilated security. Such transactions are often motivated by anxiety for immediate income recognition or by tax considerations. This practice significantly diminishes the worth, marketability, and liquidity of the securities.

Ex-coupon securities, or the stripped coupons, are distinctly different from securities that have the unmatured coupons attached. The ex-coupon security and resulting coupons:

- Have diminished and uncertain market value and impaired practical liquidity.
- Cannot be wire transferred on the Federal Reserve Communication System.
- Are not eligible for pledge against owning bank's own trust deposits.
- Are not acceptable as collateral for U.S. government deposits or borrowings from Federal Reserve banks.
- Are not, absent adequate customer disclosure, suitable for sale to customers or as repurchase agreement collateral with customers.

If an institution has engaged or elects to engage in such transactions, they must be reported as follows:

- The original purchase price must be allocated between the principal portion and the coupons at the time the security is divided. This allocation will be based upon the yield to maturity of that security at the time it was purchased by the institution.

- The profit or loss on the portion sold must be recognized during the period in which the sale occurred as "other income" or "other expense." It will be the difference between that portion of the original purchase price, allocated as above to the portion sold, and the actual selling price of that portion. The portion retained will be carried on the books of the institution at its allocated portion of the original purchase price. The amount of any discount (or premium if any) must be amortized to maturity. Detached coupons or principal portions held by a bank either as a result of purchase or of mutilating securities held for its own account will be reported as "Other notes, bonds, and debentures," and not as "U.S. Treasury securities," "Obligations of other U.S. Government agencies and corporations," or "Obligations of States and political subdivisions in the United States."

Separate Trading of Registered Interest and Principal of Securities (STRIPS) are direct obligations of the U.S. Treasury that have their principal and interest components separated. Each component part is assigned a separate CUSIP number and may be separately owned and sold. Because STRIPS are an obligation of the U.S. government, national banks may buy, sell, deal-in, or underwrite STRIPS without dollar limitation. Also, because STRIPS are maintained in book-entry form, they overcome many of the disadvantages of detached coupons and other proprietary stripped coupon derivative products such as CATS and TIGRS.

Stripped securities products such as STRIPS, CATS, TIGRS, stripped coupons and stripped bonds, and Original Issue Discount Bonds (OIDs) may have long maturities, and can exhibit extreme price volatility. Accordingly, disproportionately large (in relation to the bank's total portfolio) long-maturity holdings of zero coupon securities are unsuitable investments for banks.

Stripped Mortgage Backed Securities

Stripped Mortgage Backed Securities (SMBS) consist of two classes of securities with each class receiving a different portion of the monthly interest and principal cash flows from the underlying mortgage backed securities. In its purest form, an SMBS is converted into an interest-only (IO) strip, where the investor receives 100 percent of the interest cash flow, and a principal-only (PO) strip, where the investor receives 100 percent of the principal cash flow.

IOs and POs have volatile price characteristics based, in part, on the prepayment of the underlying mortgages and, consequently, on the maturity of the stripped security Generally, POs will increase in value when interest rates decline while IOs increase in value when interest rates rise. In theory, the purchase of an IO strip may serve to offset the interest rate risk associated with mortgages and similar instruments held by a depository institution. Similarly, a PO may be useful to offset the effect of interest rate movements on the value of mortgage servicing. However, when purchasing an IO or PO, the investor is speculating on the movement of future interest rates and how this movement will affect the prepayment of the underlying collateral. Furthermore, those SMBS that do not have the guarantee of a government agency or a government-sponsored agency as to the payment of principal and interest have an added element of credit risk.

As a general rule, SMBS cannot be considered as suitable investments for the vast majority of bank investors. Speculative positions or non-hedge positions in SMBS should not be considered as suitable investments for national banks and should be strongly criticized. SMBS, however, may be appropriate general hedges for banks that have highly sophisticated and well managed mortgage backed securities portfolios, mortgage portfolios, or mortgage banking functions. In such banks, however, the acquisition of SMBS should be undertaken only in conformance with carefully developed and documented plans prescribing specific positioning and loss limits and control arrangements for enforcing such limits. These plans should be approved by the bank's board of directors and vigorously enforced.

SMBS holdings must be accounted for in accordance with Financial Accounting Standards Board Statement 91, which requires that the carrying amount be adjusted when actual prepayment experience differs from prepayment estimates.

Residuals

Residuals are the excess of cash flows from a mortgage backed securities transaction after the payments due to the bondholders and the trust administrative expenses have been satisfied. This cash flow is extremely sensitive to prepayments, and thus has a high degree of interest-rate risk. Generally, the value of Residual interests rises when interest rates rise. Theoretically, a Residual can be used as a risk management tool to offset declines in the value of fixed rate mortgage or Mortgage Backed Securities portfolios. However, it should be understood by all residual interest purchasers that the "yield" on these instruments is inversely related to their effectiveness as a risk management vehicle. The highest yielding Residuals have limited risk management value, usually because of their complicated structure and/or unusual collateral characteristics that make modeling and understanding the economic cash flows very difficult. Alternatively, those Residuals priced for modest yields generally have positive risk management characteristics.

It is important to understand that a Residual cash flow is highly dependent upon the prepayments received. Banks should exercise caution when purchasing a Residual interest, especially higher "yielding" interests, because the associated risk may warrant an even higher return to adequately compensate the investor for the interest-rate risk assumed. Purchases of Residual interests should be supported by in-house evaluation of possible rate of return ranges in combination with varying prepayment assumptions.

Holdings of Residuals should be accounted for in the same way as stripped mortgage-backed securities and should be reported as "other assets" on regulatory reports. Speculative or non- hedge holdings of Residuals should be strongly criticized.

Resale and Repurchase Agreements

Money market instruments, usually short-term U.S. government securities, are purchased for the bank's own account or acquired under an agreement to resell and are then sold under an agreement to repurchase. The rate of interest received and paid is generally dictated by prevailing market rates. Profits are based on a modest positive spread between interest earned and interest paid. A bank may attempt to improve profits by increasing the volume of such transactions by using the proceeds of completed transactions to finance an inventory of assets to be used in further repurchase arrangements. An alternative method of increasing profits is to increase the earnings yield of the instruments employed in these transactions by lowering their quality or by lengthening their maturity.

Risks inherent in that type of repurchase transaction should be controlled by policy guidelines that:

- Establish account limits.
- Require approximately matched asset and liability maturities.
- Provide for reasonable collateral margin and valuation techniques.
- Provide for collateral custody by the bank or an independent third party acting for the bank.
- Subject the underlying securities of a resale agreement to periodic market valuation, in order to determine market exposure.
- Mandate credit approvals for parties providing securities acquired under agreements to resell.
- Insist that characteristics of the money market instruments be compatible with the bank's own investment standards.

National banks that engage in repurchase or reverse repurchase agreements are encouraged to have policies and controls to suit their particular circumstances. Banking Circular 210, dated October 31, 1985, describes minimum guidelines needed to manage credit risk exposure to counterparties under securities repurchase agreements, and for controlling the securities underlying repurchase agreement transactions. These guidelines should be followed by national banks that enter into repurchase agreements with other financial institutions or securities dealers.

Repositioning Repos

Repositioning repos are often used to fund the acquisition of depreciated "when issued" (WI), forward placement positions, "pair-off" transactions, "corporate or extended" settlement transactions, or securities otherwise being held for "gains trading."

A bank may want to commit to a large position in securities with the intent of closing-out the position by selling the securities at a profit whenever the opportunity arises. If the securities position is sufficiently large, the selling dealer may provide or arrange for repurchase agreement "financing" to complete the transaction. This type of "financing" is called a "repositioning repurchase" agreement.

In such agreements, the dealer agrees to buy back the security under an agreement to resell. In reality, the purchasing bank never remits the full purchase price to the selling dealer, instead the bank purchasing the securities remits to the funding dealer a "margin" payment which is generally equivalent to the difference between the purchase price and the current market value of the security. This type of repurchase arrangement can create serious funds management problems as variable rate source funds with short maturities are used to finance the acquisition of long maturity, fixed rate assets.

Securities dealers are interested in arranging repurchase financing for several reasons:

- In a forward-contract or security-purchase commitment, such as a WI or pair-off transaction, no money has been exchanged. In the absence of a repurchase agreement, if the financial institution decides to cancel or back-out of the transaction rather than take a loss, the selling dealer will have to absorb the loss and/or bring suit to enforce the contract.

- The purchaser can acquire a large amount of securities in exchange for a comparatively small margin payment. This results in more commission-fee income for the selling dealer.

- A repositioning repo "locks-in" the customer/dealer relationship. The financial institution must then provide its own financing and probably recognize a loss if it wishes to sever its relationship with the dealer.

- Once the concept of repositioning repos or leverage financing of securities is accepted by the financial institution, there is virtually no limit to the amount of securities a dealer can conceivably sell to the customer bank.

Repositioning repos are considered unsafe and unsound as a means of funding investment portfolio activities because:

- They are the result of speculative securities transactions.

- During periods of rising interest rates, they are used as a method of loss avoidance. That is, if the securities purchase position can be sold and settled at a profit, the bank does so. However, if the purchased securities can only be sold and settled at a loss, the securities are recorded and carried in the bank's investment portfolio at cost, and financed via repurchase agreement.

- A financial institution usually does not enter into a simultaneous purchase and repositioning repo transaction unless the underlying security is depreciated or funds are not available from more traditional sources at competitive rates. As interest rates increase, bond prices decrease.

As depreciation continues to increase, the practical liquidity of portfolio holdings is eroded and capital funds are impaired at the same time that interest earnings and expense spreads are diminishing.

Securities acquired and funded via repositioning repos are to be regarded as trading account holdings or securities held for resale and recorded on a mark to market, or lower of cost or market basis.

Repo to Maturity

A repo to maturity is often used in a rising or high interest rate environment when bond prices are depressed. A securities dealer offers to purchase securities from a bank under agreement to resell provided the bank uses the repo proceeds to purchase additional bonds from the securities dealer. To induce the banker to enter into the transaction, the repo rate is usually set lower than prevailing repo rates. The dealer immediately sells the securities thereby incurring no cost-of- carry or market risk. The bank and the dealer agree to continue the repo arrangement until the repoed bond matures.

Repos to maturity are considered unsafe and unsound because:

- The intent of the transaction is to permanently dispose of a depreciated bank asset rather than enter into a short term borrowing arrangement. Hence, the bank avoids the recognition of a loss on the sale of a depreciated security

- The proceeds of the funds generated from the repo arrangement are used to purchase additional securities at a price that may be inflated, thereby inflating the balance sheet and providing a "built-in" depreciation in the investment portfolio. The depreciation or unrealized loss erodes the practical liquidity of the investment portfolio and threatens capital funds.

- The purchase of bonds at inflated prices, if done with the knowledge of bank officers, may be construed as willful misstatement of bank records and regulatory reports.

Dollar Repos and Dollar Rolls

A dollar repurchase agreement (dollar repo) is a transaction involving the sale of a mortgage-backed security (MBS) from an investment portfolio and the simultaneous forward purchase of a different but similar MBS within a specified time and at a specified price. Fixed-coupon and yield maintenance dollar repos are the most common types of dollar repo agreements. Both kinds of dollar repos involve the contemporaneous sale and commitment to repurchase the same types of MBSs with approximately the same maturity and outstanding principal. In a fixed-coupon agreement, the seller and purchaser agree that delivery will be made with a MBS having the same coupon as the security sold. In a yield-maintenance agreement, the parties agree that delivery will be made with a security with a different coupon but at a price that will provide the seller with a yield that is specified in the agreement. Yield maintenance dollar repos are always considered to be sales and purchases and require a current recordation of gains and losses.

At the start of a fixed-coupon dollar repo, the bank sells the security to the dealer, and the security is no longer registered in the bank's name. Although the portfolio holding has been sold and delivered-out, there is no adjustment of the portfolio records to reflect the sale of the security or the gain or loss on the sale of the portfolio holding. In fact, all accounting within the portfolio continues as if the bank still owns the security. The bank receives no principal or interest payments on the security during the dollar repo agreement's term. When the substantially identical security underlying the forward placement contract is delivered to the bank, it is substituted for the security still being carried on the books, but sold under agreement to repurchase. The security to be purchased is typically on a "to be announced" (TBA) basis, meaning the pools of mortgages to collateralize the purchased security have been formed but not specifically identified.

Under Generally Accepted Accounting Principles (GAAP), the fixed-coupon dollar repo transaction is reported as a security sold under agreement to repurchase (a financing) and not as a sale. This is because, from the accounting profession's point of view, the sale and contemporaneous purchase of a similar security is a "wash" transaction that should not be recognized as a sale. However, cash taken in on the sale needs to be recognized along with the liability to purchase the similar security.

Banks often consider dollar repos as another source of funding and execute them whenever their cost is estimated to be less than other types of funding. However, during a period of rising interest rates, dollar repos can also be used to sell depreciated securities in a manner that avoids recognizing the loss that normally occurs if the transaction is accounted for as a sale of a bank asset.

Securities dealers can use dollar repo arrangements to deliver a different but similar security as a way to profit from the differences in prices between the instruments being sold and purchased. This practice, commonly referred to as "worst delivery," involves obtaining a relatively expensive MBS from the seller, and delivering the cheapest security obtainable in the current market to the seller at the dollar repo's maturity. Although the cheapest security has the same coupon interest rate as the sold security, its expected prepayment characteristics may be different, and create the price differential. In a rising interest rate environment, it will probably be cheaper to purchase and deliver a mortgage-backed security with a slow prepayment history. In this situation, the investor will continue to receive the same coupon rate on the principal of the security but will be unable to reinvest the prepaid principal of the security at higher current rates as rapidly as an investor holding a security with a faster repayment history. Dealers will also take seasoned securities from the bank but deliver securities without a prepayment record, such as TBAs. The securities without payment histories typically sell for less than seasoned securities with an established, favorable payment history. Dealers active in the dollar repo market study the history of mortgage pool prepayments to take advantage of these differences.

Fixed-coupon dollar repos represent transactions that must involve substantially identical MBSs. The following guidelines must be observed if fixed-coupon dollar repo transactions are to be considered a financing. MBSs are judged to be substantially identical only when all of the following criteria are met:

- The securities are collateralized by similar mortgages (e.g., single-family residential mortgages for single-family residential mortgages).

- The replacement security is issued by the same entity that issued the original security and must be identical in form and type (e.g., GNMA I for GNMA I).

- The securities have the same original stated term to maturity (e.g., 30 years), and the expected remaining life is nearly identical.

- The securities have identical coupon interest rates.

- The securities have approximately the same market yield.

- The aggregate principal amounts of MBSs given up and MBSs forward purchased in the transaction are within industry- established parameters for good delivery. The Public Securities Association (PSA) currently defines good delivery as a 2.5 percent gain or loss in aggregate principal amounts.

The following conditions must also be met.

- The bank must own the MBS and hold it in its portfolio for a reasonable period of time. The minimum holding period for the security is the number of days to the next issuance date of the MBS by the issuing agency (generally 30 days).

- The settlement term on the dollar repo cannot exceed 12 months from the initial transaction date.

If any of those criteria are not met, the transaction should be accounted for as a sale and the forward purchase of MBSs rather than as a financing. Thereafter, the forward position should be marked to market at each reporting date until the securities are reacquired.

A dollar roll is an extension of a dollar repo. It occurs when a bank decides not to accept delivery of a fixed-coupon MBS at the repurchase date but rather "rolls it forward" by means of another sale and forward purchase transaction in which the position is offset and extended for another specified period of time. Typically, to the extent the market value of the fixed- coupon security has increased or decreased in value from the original sale date to the roll date, the bank will pay or receive payment for such price fluctuations.

Once the roll period commences, the rolled fixed-coupon dollar repo continues to be accounted for as a financing when:

- Within 12 months from the date of the initial sell and forward buy transaction, the bank must accept delivery, close out its forward position, fund and place the MBS in its investment portfolio. For future dollar repos using these reacquired securities to be accounted for as financings, the security must be acquired and remain in the bank's possession at least until the next issuance date of the MBS (generally 30 days). The funding for the retention of the security for this holding period must come from a source independent of the securities transactions, such as deposits or federal funds lines. This mandatory delivery condition is intended to demonstrate the bank's ability to fund the purchase of the securities and its intent to hold them for investment.

- At all times during the rollover or extension period, the bank must be able to demonstrate its ability to fund the reacquisition of the MBSs and close out its forward position.

If the above conditions are not met, the transaction must be accounted for as a sale and purchase of MBSs rather than as a financing, starting with the month the ability of the bank to fund the delivery of the securities has not been demonstrated or at the end of the 12-month period, whichever comes first. Thereafter, the forward position must be marked to market at each reporting date until the MBSs are reacquired.

Bank dealers who conduct dollar repos and rolls should not account for these transactions as financings. They should be recorded on a cash or forward basis as purchases and sales.

Securities Lending

A national bank may lend its own investment securities or trading account securities. National banks may also lend customers' securities held in custody, safekeeping, trust, or pension accounts to a third party pursuant to a written agreement with the customer. Securities dealers and commercial banks are the primary borrowers of securities. They borrow securities to cover securities fails (securities sold but not available for delivery), short sales, and option and arbitrage positions.

Securities lending is conducted through open ended "loan" agreements, which may be terminated on short notice by the lender or borrower. The borrower of the securities pays a fee to the owner of the securities. A bank lending customer securities will share in the fee income generated by loaning the securities. The objective of such lending is to receive a safe return in addition to the normal interest or dividends received from the securities. Securities loans are collateralized with cash, U.S. government or federal agency securities, or letters of credit. At the outset, each loan is collateralized at a predetermined margin. If the market value of the collateral falls below the predetermined acceptable level while a loan is outstanding, a margin call is made by the lender institution. If a loan becomes over-collateralized because of appreciation of collateral or market depreciation of a loaned security, the borrower usually has the opportunity to request the return of any excessive margin.

When a securities loan is terminated, the securities are returned to the lender and the collateral to the borrower. Fees received on securities loans are divided between the lender institution and the customer account that owns the securities. In situations involving cash collateral, part of the interest earned on the temporary investment of cash is returned to the borrower and the remainder is divided between the lender institution and the customer account that owns the securities.

All national banks that participate in securities lending should establish written policies and procedures governing these activities. OCC Banking Circular 196, dated May 7, 1985, discusses the minimum acceptable topics to be covered by the written policies and procedures.

Government Securities Act Requirements

Specific provisions of the Government Securities Act (GSA) apply to all national banks, including those with limited government securities activities that are exempt from filing a notice as a Government Securities Broker-Dealer with the OCC. The provisions of the GSA that apply to all national banks include: (a) national banks that engage in repurchase transactions with customers while retaining custody or control of the subject government securities; and (b) all depository institutions that hold government securities for customers. The following discussion does not apply to the additional provisions of the GSA regulations concerning national banks that are required to file as government securities broker-dealers (See Section 204).

Except for Part 450, (custodial holdings of securities by depository institutions) the definition of U.S. government security includes: U.S. Treasury obligations, as well as obligations of the Government National Mortgage Association (GNMA), the Federal National Mortgage Association (FNMA), the Federal Home Loan Mortgage Corporation (FHLMC), and the Student Loan Marketing Association (SLMA). Options on these securities are also considered to be government securities for all parts of the regulations.

Hold-in-Custody Repurchase Agreements

All national banks that retain custody of securities sold under an agreement to repurchase must comply with the requirements for hold-in-custody repurchase agreements described in 17 CFR 403.5(d). For purposes of the GSA, a national bank is also considered to be retaining custody of the repurchase agreement securities when the securities are maintained through an account at another institution (e.g., a correspondent bank or the local Federal Reserve Bank) and the securities continue to be under the control of the national bank.

The following requirements apply to all hold-in-custody repurchase agreements:

- Hold-in-custody repurchase agreements must be transacted pursuant to a written repurchase agreement (see 17 CFR 403.5(d)(1)(i)).

- If the customer agrees to allow substitution of securities in a hold-in-custody repurchase transaction, then authority for the national bank to substitute securities must be contained in the written repurchase agreement (see 17 CFR 403.5(d)(1)(iv)).

- Where the national bank reserves the right to substitute securities, a specific disclosure statement as written into the regulation must be prominently displayed in the written repurchase agreement immediately preceding the provision allowing the right to substitute. No editing or paraphrasing of the required language is permitted under the regulations, with the exception that substitution of other terms for the words buyer and seller (which are bracketed in the disclosure statement) may be used.

- A national bank issuing a hold-in-custody repurchase agreement must disclose to the customer in writing that the funds held pursuant to a repurchase agreement are not a deposit, and, therefore, not insured by the Federal Deposit Insurance Corporation (see 17 CFR 403.5(d)(1)(iii)).

- Written confirmations describing the specific securities subject to the transaction must be sent to the customer by close of business on the day the transaction is initiated, as well as on any day on which substitution of securities occurs (see 17 CFR 403.5(d)(1)(ii).

- Confirmations must identify the specific securities by issuer, maturity, coupon, par amount, market value, and CUSIP or mortgage pool number of the underlying securities (see 17 CFR 403.5(d)(2)(i)).

The frequency or short duration of a particular type of transaction, such as an overnight repurchase agreement or a daily "sweep" of a customer's deposits into a hold-in-custody repurchase transaction, does not eliminate the requirement for a financial institution to send a prompt and accurate confirmation to the customer.

Pooling of securities as collateral for repurchase agreements is no longer permitted. "Blind pooled" hold-in-custody repurchase transactions occur when a seller does not deliver securities and does not identify specific securities as belonging to a specific customer. Instead, the bank sets aside, or otherwise designates, a pool of securities to collateralize its outstanding repurchase obligations. The regulations require that the written confirmation sent to a customer must identify the specific securities that are the subject of the hold-in-custody repurchase transaction. A specific security identified to a customer must be in an authorized denomination, that is, in a deliverable par amount.

The regulations do not require written agreements for repurchase transactions where the securities are delivered to the customer or to another depository acting pursuant to a tripartite agreement with the financial institution and the customer.

Custodial Holdings of Government Securities

All national banks that hold or safekeep U.S. government securities for customers must comply with 17 CFR 450. These regulations apply when a national bank holds the customers' securities directly or maintains the customers' securities through another institution.

The Department of the Treasury has determined that the rules and standards of the Comptroller of the Currency applying to government securities held in a fiduciary capacity are adequate to meet the requirements of this regulation. Thus, a national bank will be exempt from Part 450 requirements provided two conditions are met. The depository institution must adopt policies and procedures that subject the custodial holdings to all the requirements of 12 CFR 9. Also, such custodial holdings must be subject to examination by the OCC for compliance with these fiduciary requirements, (see 17 CFR 450.3 (a)(1) and (2)).

To comply with the custodial holding requirements of Part 450, depository institutions must observe the following requirements.

- All government securities held for customers, including those subject to repurchase agreements with customers, must be segregated from the depository's own assets and kept free from lien of any third party granted or created by the depository (see 17 CFR 450.4 (a)(1)).

- A depository institution that holds securities for a customer through another institution ("custodian institution") must notify the custodian institution that the securities are customer securities (see 17 CFR 450.4(a)(2)(i)(A)).

- The custodian institution must maintain the customer securities in an account that is designated for customers of the depository institution, and that does not contain proprietary securities of the depository (see 17 CFR 450.4 (a)(2)(i)(B)).

- The depository institution must notify the custodian institution that these securities are to remain free of any lien, charge, or claim in favor of the custodian or any persons attempting to make a claim through the custodian (see 17 CFR 450.4(a)(2)(i)(C)). The custodian institution upon receiving such notice from the depository institution, is required to treat these securities as customer securities and maintain them in compliance with Section 450.4.

- When holding customer securities for a depository, the custodian institution does not have to keep records that identify individual customers of the depository, unless the custodian institution is acting directly on behalf of the customer, such as in a tripartite repurchase agreement transaction (see 17 450.4(e)).

When a depository institution maintains customer securities in an account at a Federal Reserve bank, it is deemed to be in compliance with requirements to hold customer securities free of lien if any lien of the FED, or other party claiming through it, expressly excludes customer securities. The depository institution is not required to maintain customer securities in a separate custody account at the FED, although, such segregation is encouraged. However, the depository institution must segregate the customers' securities on its own records and observe the following recordkeeping requirements.

- A depository institution safekeeping U.S. government securities for customers must issue to the customer a confirmation or safekeeping receipt for each government security held (see 17 CFR 450 (b)(1)).

- The confirmation or safekeeping receipt must identify the issuer, maturity date, par amount, and coupon rate of the security being confirmed (see 17 CFR 450 (b)(1)).

- A records system of government securities held for customers must be maintained separate and distinct from other records of the depository institution (see 17 CFR 450.4(c)).

- These records must:

- identify each customer and each government security held for a customer;
- describe the customer's interest in the security and;
- indicate all receipts and deliveries of securities and cash in connection with the securities.

• A copy of the safekeeping receipt or confirmation given to customers must be maintained.

• This system of records must provide an adequate basis for audit (see 17 CFR 450.4(c))(1-5)).

• The required records for Part 450 must be maintained in an easily accessible place for at least two years and not disposed of for at least six years (see 17 CFR 450.4(f)).

• The depository institution providing customer safekeeping is required to conduct a count of physical securities and securities held in book-entry form at least annually (see 17 CFR 450.4(d)).

• In order to count securities held outside of the depository, such as book-entry securities held at a Federal Reserve Bank, the depository must reconcile its records with those of the outside custodian (see 17 CFR 450.4(d)(1)).

• The depository institution responsible for the count must verify any securities in transfer, in transit, pledged, loaned, borrowed, deposited, failed to receive or deliver, or subject to a repurchase or reverse repurchase agreement, when the securities have been out of the depository's possession for longer than 30 days (see 17 CFR 450.4(d)(2))

• The dates and results of the counts and reconcilements must be documented within seven days of the required count, with the differences in securities counts noted (see 17 CFR 450.4(d)(3)).

International Division Investments

This section discusses money market investments and securities purchased by the bank's international division and overseas branches for its own account.

Securities purchased primarily for resale to customers, i.e., trading account securities, are seldom encountered in a bank's international division or overseas branches, but when they are found, the procedures in the "Bank Dealer Activities" section apply. International securities trading is normally conducted in foreign affiliates, which are regulated by the Federal Reserve Board and are subject to 12 CFR 211 (Regulation K).

The same types of "money market" instruments exist in international banking as in domestic banking. They include short-term credit terms, such as commercial paper, other bankers' acceptances purchased, negotiable certificates of deposit, and assets purchased or sold under repurchase agreements. In some banks, such instruments are handled by either international division officers or, in certain instances, by a separate international investment department. In other banks they are handled by the bank's domestic investment officer. If the international examination is made in conjunction with the domestic examination, the examiners should decide together who will review money market holdings as well as investment activities. Usually, domestic examiners review the overall maturity position, earnings versus risk considerations, federal income tax aspects, and overall risk diversification factors of international division investments as they relate to the overall condition of the bank's investment securities department.

Investments held by most international divisions predominately represent securities issued by various governmental entities of the countries in which the bank's foreign branches are located. Such investments are held for a variety of purposes:

- They are required by various local laws.
- They are used to meet foreign reserve requirements.
- They result in reduced tax liabilities.
- They enable the bank to use new or increased rediscount facilities or benefit from greater deposit or lending authorities.
- They are used by the bank as an expression of "good-will" toward a country.

The examiner should be familiar with the applicable sections of 12 CFR 211 (Regulation K) regarding a national bank's holdings abroad as well as other regulations discussed in this section.

Because of mandatory investment requirements by some countries, those securities held cannot always be as "liquid" and "readily marketable" as required in domestic banking. However, the amount of "mandatory" holdings normally will represent only a relatively small amount of the bank's total investments or capital funds.

A bank's international division may also hold securities strictly for investment purposes which are expected to provide a reasonable rate of return commensurate with safety. As with domestic investment securities, safety must take precedence, followed by liquidity and marketability. Such securities are liquid if their maturities are short and there is assurance that they will be paid at maturity. They are marketable if they can be sold in a very short time period at a price commensurate with yield and quality. As with domestic banking, speculation in marginal foreign securities to generate more favorable yields is an unsound banking practice and should be discouraged.

Generally, banks are prohibited from investing in stocks. However, a number of exceptions are detailed in this handbook that are often applicable to the international division. For example, the bank may hold stock in overseas corporations that hold title to foreign bank premises (12 USC 371d and 12 CFR 7.3100). Both stock and other securities holdings as required by various laws of a particular country in which the bank maintains a branch are permitted in unlimited amounts under 12 CFR 211.3 (Foreign Branches of Member Banks). Other sections of 12 CFR 211 permit the bank to acquire and hold, directly or indirectly, stock in foreign banks subject to certain limitations.

For foreign securities authorized for investment purposes under 12 USC 24(7), Standard and Poor's, Moody's, and other U.S. rating service publications rate Canadian and other selected foreign securities. However, in many other countries, securities rating services are limited or non-existent. When they do exist, the ratings are only indicative and should be supplemented by additional information regarding legality, credit soundness, marketability, foreign exchange, and country risk factors. Local attorneys' opinions are often the best source of determining whether a particular foreign security has the full faith and credit backing of a country's government.

Sufficient analytical data must be provided to allow the bank's board of directors and senior management to make informed judgments regarding the effectiveness of the international division's investment policy and procedures. The international investment portfolio should be reviewed at least annually, by the board of directors, and quarterly, by senior management to assure adherence to written policies and procedures.

Investment Securities
(Section 203)

1. Complete or update the Investment Securities section of the Internal Control Questionnaire.

2. Based on the evaluation of internal controls and the work performed by internal/external auditors (see separate program), determine the scope of the examination.

3. Test for compliance with policies, practices, procedures, and internal controls in conjunction with performing the following examination procedures. Also, obtain a listing of any deficiencies noted in the latest review done by internal/external auditors from the examiner assigned "Internal and External Audits," and determine if corrections have been accomplished.

   a. Determine the extent and effectiveness of investment policy supervision by:

      • Reviewing the abstracted minutes of the board of directors and/or appropriate committee minutes.
      • Determining that proper authorizations have been made for investment officers or committees.
      • Determine that there are proper authorizations, restrictions, and limitations on the delegation of investment portfolio authorities to nonaffiliated institutions or to non-employees.
      • Determine that the board has approved securities dealers with whom the bank transacts business.
      • Evaluating the sufficiency of analytical data used by the board or investment committee.
      • Reviewing the reporting methods used by department supervisors and internal auditors to insure compliance with established policy.
      • Preparing a memo for the examiner assigned "Duties and Responsibilities of Directors" and the examiner in charge of the international examination, if applicable, stating conclusions on the effectiveness of directors' supervision of the domestic and/or

international division investment policy. All conclusions should be documented.

4.   Perform appropriate verification procedures.

5.   Obtain the following:

    a. Trial balances of investment account holdings and money market instruments, such as commercial paper, bankers' acceptances, negotiable certificates of deposit, securities purchased under agreements to resell, and federal funds sold.

    b. A list of any assets carried in loans and discounts on which interest is exempt from federal income taxes and which are carried in the investment account on Call Reports.

    c. A list of open purchase and sale commitments.

    d. A schedule of all securities, forward placement contracts, futures contracts, and standby contracts purchased and/or sold since the last examination.

    e. A maturity schedule of securities sold under repurchase agreements.

    f. A list of pledged assets and secured liabilities.

    g. A list of the names and addresses of all securities dealers doing business with the bank.

    h. A list of all U.S. Government guaranteed loans which are recorded and carried as an investment account security.

    i. For international division and overseas branches, a list of investments:

- Held to comply with various foreign governmental regulations requiring such investments.
- Used to meet foreign reserve requirements.
- Required as stock exchange guarantees or used to enable the bank

to provide securities services.

- Representing investment of surplus funds.
- Used to obtain telephone and telex services.
- Representing club and school memberships.
- Acquired through debts previously contracted.
- Representing minority interests in nonaffiliated companies.
- Held for other purposes.
- Representing trading account securities.

6.   Using updated data available from reports of condition, NBSS printouts, investment advisor, and correspondent bank portfolio analysis reports, obtain or prepare an analysis of investment and money market holdings that includes:

a. A month-by-month schedule of par, book, and market value of issues maturing in 1 year.

b. Schedules of par, book, and market values of holdings in the liquidity segment and the permanent, or investment for income, segment of the investment portfolio. Those schedules should be indexed by maturity date. The schedule should be detailed by maturity dates over the following time periods: 1 to 2 years, 3 to 5 years, 6 to 10 years, 11 to 20 years, and over 20 years.

c. A schedule of book or par values of municipal and corporate holdings by rating classifications.

d. Book value totals of holdings by obligor or industry, related obligors or industries, geographic distribution, yield, and special characteristics, such as moral obligations, conversion, or warrant features.

e. Par value schedules of Type I, II and III investment holdings, by those legally defined types.

f. For the international division, totals (U.S. $ equivalents) of holdings by:

- Total portfolio (book and market values).
- Name of issuer (par value).

- Issuer's country of domicile (book value).
- Interest rate (book and par value).
- Pledged securities (market value).

7. Review the reconcilement of investment and money market account(s) trial balances to general ledger control account(s).

8. Using an appropriate sampling technique, select from the trial balance(s) municipal investments and money market holdings for examination. If transaction volume permits, include all securities purchased since the last general examination in the population of items to be reviewed. If verification steps are to be performed, use the same population.

(Before continuing, refer to steps 16 through 18. They should be performed in conjunction with steps 9 through 15. International division holdings should be reviewed with domestic holdings to ensure compliance when combined, with applicable legal requirements.)

9. Perform the following procedures for each investment and money market holding selected in step 8.

    a. Check appropriate legal opinions or published data outlining legal status.

    b. If market prices are provided to the bank by an independent party (excludes affiliates and securities dealers selling investments to the bank), or if they are independently tested as a documented part of the bank's audit program, those prices should be accepted. If the independence of the prices cannot be established, test market values by reference to one of the following sources:

        - Published quotations.
        - Appraisals by outside pricing services.

    c. If market prices are provided by the bank and cannot be verified by reference to published quotations or other sources, test those prices by using the "comparative yield method" to calculate approximate yield to maturity:

Approximate Yield to Maturity =

$$\frac{\text{Annual Interest} + \dfrac{\text{Par Value} - \text{Book Value}}{\text{Number of Years to Maturity}}}{1/2 \text{ (Bank Provided Market Price} + \text{Par Value)}}$$

- Compare the bank provided market price and the examiner calculated approximate yield to maturity to an independent publicly offered yield or market price for a similar type of investment with similar rating, trading volume, and maturity or call characteristics.
- Compare non-rated issues to fourth rated (BBB, Baa) bonds.
- Investigate market value variances in excess of 5 percent.

d. For investments and money market obligations in the sample that are rated, compare the ratings provided to the most recent published ratings.

10. Perform credit analysis of:

a. The obligors on securities purchased under agreements to resell, when the readily marketable value of the securities is not sufficient to satisfy the obligation or when collateral custody procedures are inadequate to assure the bank's unassailable right to the collateral.

b. All nonrated securities and money market instruments selected in step 8 or acquired since the last examination. (Consider using grading sheet contained in the appendix of this handbook.)

c. All previously detailed or currently known speculative issues.

d. All defaulted issues.

e. Any issues contained in the current Interagency Country Exposure Review Committee credit schedule obtained from the international loan portfolio manager by:

- Comparing the schedule to the foreign securities trial balance obtained in step 5 to ascertain which foreign securities are to be included in Interagency County Exposure Review Committee credits.

- For each security so identified, transcribing the following appropriate information to a separate examiner's line sheet or a related examiner's credit line sheet:
  - Amount (and U.S. dollar equivalents if a foreign currency) to include par, book, and market values.
  - How and when acquired.
  - Maturity date(s).
  - Default date, if appropriate.
  - Any pertinent comments.
- Returning schedule and appropriate examiner's line sheet(s) to the examiner assigned "International Loan Portfolio Management." No further examination procedures are necessary for these items.

11. Classify speculative and defaulted issues according to the following standards (except those securities in the Interagency Country Exposure Review and FFIEC uniform classifications of municipal securities):

a. The entire book value of speculative grade municipal general obligation securities which are not in default will be classified substandard. Market depreciation on other speculative issues should be classified doubtful. The remaining book value usually is classified substandard.

b. The entire book value of all defaulted municipal general obligation securities will be classified doubtful. Market depreciation on other defaulted bonds should be classified loss. The remaining book value usually is classified substandard.

c. Market depreciation on non-exempt stock should be classified loss.

d. Report comments should include:

- Description of issue.
- How and when each issue was acquired.
- Default date, if appropriate.
- Date interest paid to.
- Rating at time of acquisition.
- Comments supporting the classification.

12. Review the bank's maturity program by:

a. Reviewing the maturity schedules:

- Compare book and market values and, after considering the gain or loss on year-to-date sales, determine if the costs of selling intermediate and long-term issues appear prohibitive.
- Determine if recent acquisitions show a trend toward lengthened or shortened maturities. Discuss such trends with management.

b. Reviewing the pledged asset and secured liability schedules and isolating pledged securities by maturity segment (such as liquidity account and investment account). Then determine the market value of securities pledged in excess of net secured liabilities.

c. Reviewing the schedule of securities sold under repurchase agreement and determining if:

- Financing for securities purchases is provided via repurchase agreement by the securities dealer who originally sold the security to the bank.
- Funds acquired through the sale of securities under agreement to repurchase are invested in money market assets or if short- term repurchase agreements are being used to fund longer term, fixed rate assets.
- The extent of matched asset repo and liability repo maturities and the overall effect on liquidity resulting from unmatched positions.
- The interest rate paid on securities sold under agreement to repurchase is appropriate relative to current money market rates.
- The repurchase agreement is at the option of the buying or selling bank.

d. Reviewing the list of open purchase and sale commitments and determining the effect of their completion on maturity scheduling.

e. Submitting investment portfolio information regarding the credit quality and practical liquidity of the investment portfolio to the examiner assigned "Funds Management."

13. If the bank is engaged in dollar repos or rolls:

a. Review policies and ensure that bank practice complies with written controls and:

- Determine whether the board has approved the use of dollar repos.
- Ensure that the board has authorized particular individuals to conduct dollar repos and that they have sufficient knowledge to do so properly.
- Determine if the bank has established dollar repo credit policy guidelines and if initial and periodic credit and reputation analysis of counterparties is conducted by the bank's credit division.

b. Review management's analysis of funding sources to determine if dollar repos were found to be the least expensive type of funding for the desired time period.

c. Ensure that all yield maintenance dollar repos are treated as purchases and sales. If fixed-coupon dollar repos are recorded as financing transactions, determine that the securities returned are substantially identical to those sold by meeting the following criteria. If these criteria are not met, ensure that the forward position is marked to market monthly until the securities are reacquired and that:

- The securities are collateralized by similar types of mortgages.
- The replacement securities are issued by the same entity that issued the initial security and are identical in form and type.
- The securities have the same original stated term to maturity and their expected remaining lives are nearly identical.
- The securities have identical coupon interest rates.
- The securities have approximately the same market yield.
- The aggregate principal amounts of mortgage-backed securities (MBS) sold, and MBSs forward purchased involved in the transaction are within industry-established parameters for good delivery. The Public Securities Association (PSA) currently defines good delivery as a 2.5 percent gain or loss difference in the aggregate principal amounts.
- The settlement term of the dollar repo does not exceed 12 months from the initial transaction date.

- The bank has owned the MBS for the minimum period until the next issuance date of the MBS by the agency (generally 30 days) before employing it in a dollar repo.

d. If the bank treats dollar rolls as financing transactions, ensure that the following criteria are met. If the conditions below are not met, the transaction must be accounted for as a sale and purchase of MBSs rather than as a financing, as soon as the bank demonstrates the inability to fund or exceeds the 12-month period, whichever comes first.

- Within 12 months of the initial dollar repo, the bank must accept delivery of the security and retain it for the minimum period until the next issuance date of the MBS (generally 30 days). The funding for the security during this holding period must come from a source independent of the securities transactions, such as deposits or Fed fund lines.
- At all times during the rollover period, the bank must be able to demonstrate its ability to fund the reacquisition of the MBSs and close out its forward position.

14. Provide to the examiner assigned "Funds Management":

- Information necessary to prepare the "Ability to Meet Short- Term Funding Needs Analysis Schedule," including:
  - Market value of unpledged government and federal agency securities maturing within one year.
  - Market value of other unpledged government and federal agency securities that would be sold without loss.
  - Market value of unpledged municipal securities maturing within one year.
  - Par value of money market instruments, such as bankers acceptances, commercial paper, and certificates of deposit. (Provide amounts for each category.)
  - Commitments to purchase securities, including a description of the security, the purchase price, and the settlement date.
- Information necessary to prepare the "Rate Sensitivity Analysis Schedule," including:
  - Month-by-month maturity schedule of investments for a one- year period.

     — Month-by-month maturity schedule of money market instruments.

15. Determine whether the bank's investment policies and practices are satisfactorily balancing earnings and risk considerations by:

    a. Using NBSS or average call report data to calculate investments as a percentage of total assets, average yields on U.S. government and nontaxable investments, and:

- Comparing results to peer group statistics.
- Determining the reasons for significant variances from the norm.
- Determining if trends are apparent and the reasons for such trends.

    b. Calculating current market depreciation as a percentage of gross capital funds.

    c. Reviewing the analysis of municipal and corporate issues by rating classification and:

- Determining the total in each rating class and the total of non-rated issues.
- Determining the total of non-rated investment securities issued by obligors located outside of the bank's service area (exclude U.S. government guaranteed issues).
- Reviewing acquisitions since the prior examination and ascertaining reasons for trends that may suggest a shift in the rated quality of investment holdings.

    d. Reviewing coupon rates or yields (when available) and comparing those recently acquired investments and money market holdings with coupon rates or yields that appear high, or low, to similarly acquired instruments of analogous types, ratings, and maturity characteristics. Discuss significant rate or yield variances with management.

    e. Reviewing schedule of securities, futures and forward placement contracts, purchased and sold since the last examination and determining whether the volume of trading is consistent with policy objectives.

f. If the majority of sales resulted in gains, determining if profit-taking is consistent with stated policy objectives or is motivated by anxiety for short-term income.

g. Determining whether the bank has discounted or has plans to discount future investment income by selling interest coupons in advance of interest payment dates.

h. Reviewing the list of commitments to purchase or sell investments or money market instruments. Determine the effect of completion of these contracts on future earnings.

16. Review the bank's federal income tax position, and:

a. Determine, by discussion with appropriate officer(s), if the bank is taking advantage of procedures to minimize tax liability in view of other investment objectives.

b. Review or compute actual and budgeted:

- Tax exempt holdings as a percentage of total assets.
- Applicable income taxes as a percentage of net operating income before taxes.

c. Discuss with management the tax implications of losses resulting from securities sales.

17. Determine that proper risk diversification exists within the portfolio by:

a. Reviewing totals of holdings by single obligor or industry, related obligors or industries, geographic distribution, yields, and securities that have special characteristics (include individual due from bank accounts from the list received from the examiner assigned "Due From Banks" and all money market instruments), and:

- Detail, as concentrations, all holdings equalling 25 percent or more of capital funds.
- List all holdings equalling at least 10 percent but less than 25 percent of capital funds and submit that information to the

examiner assigned "Loan Portfolio Management." These holdings will be combined with any additional advances in the lending areas.

b. Performing a credit analysis of all non-rated holdings determined to be a concentration if not performed in step 10.

18. If the bank is engaged in financial futures, forward placement, or standby contracts, determine if:

- The policy is specific enough to outline permissible contract strategies and their relationships to other banking activities.
- Recordkeeping systems are sufficiently detailed to permit a determination of whether operating personnel have acted in accordance with authorized objectives.
- The board of directors or its designee has established specific contract position limits, and reviews contract positions at least monthly to ascertain conformance with those limits.
- Gross and net positions are within authorized positions and limits, and if trades were executed by persons authorized to trade futures.
- The bank maintains general ledger memorandum accounts or commitment registers which, at a minimum, include:
  - The type and amount of each contract.
  - The maturity date of each contract.
  - The current market price and cost of each contract.
  - The amount held in margin accounts.
- All futures contracts and forward and standby contracts are revalued on the basis of market or the lower of cost or market at each month-end.
- Securities acquired as the result of completed contracts are valued at the lower of cost or market upon settlement.
- Fee income received by the bank on stand-by contracts is accounted for properly.
- Financial reports disclose futures, forwards, and stand-by activity.
- The bank has instituted a system for monitoring credit risk exposure in forward and stand-by contract activity.
- The bank's internal controls, management reports, and audit procedures are adequate to assure adherence to policy.

- The bank has submitted a notice of intent to the Deputy Comptroller (District).

19. If the bank is engaged in financial futures, forward placement, or standby contracts, determine if the contracts have a reasonable correlation to the bank's business needs and capacity to fulfill its obligations under the contracts by:

  - Comparing the contract commitment and maturity dates to the anticipated offset.
  - Reporting significant gaps to the examiner assigned "Funds Management."
  - Comparing the amounts of outstanding contracts to the amounts of the anticipated offset.
  - Ascertaining the extent of the correlation between expected interest rate movements on the contracts and the anticipated offset.
  - Determining the effect of the loss recognition on future earnings and, if significant, reporting it to the examiner assigned "Analytical Review of Income and Expense."

20. If the bank is engaged in financial futures contract trading activity, determine whether:

  - The board of directors specifically approved written policies about nonhedging futures contract strategies.
  - Nonhedging uses of futures contracts only takes place in bank dealer units.
  - Bank participation is limited to contracts on instruments in which the bank is authorized to and does in fact deal.
  - Futures contract positions used for nonhedging purposes are limited to amounts that do not exceed trade date position limits on related cash instruments.
  - Aggregate bank-wide positions in any futures contract do not exceed a reasonable percentage of the total "open interest" in a contract month, consistent with safe and soundness considerations.
  - Controls, limits, and accounting procedures are established (see BC-79) with appropriate tests to evaluate the nonhedging program on an ongoing basis.

21. If the bank owns shares of mutual funds or unit investment trusts, review the prospectuses and call reports to:

    a. Determine if the investment companies' portfolios consist solely of obligations eligible for purchase by national banks for their own account pursuant to 12 USC 24(7).

    b. Determine whether the bank's investment in shares of investment companies, whose portfolios contain investments subject to the limits of 12 USC 24 or 84, does not exceed 10 percent of its capital and surplus for each investment company Check for violations of the 10 percent limitation of 12 USC 24(7) because of the bank's cumulative holdings of a particular security in the portfolios of more than one investment company, or in combination with the bank's direct holdings.

    c. Determine whether investment companies using futures, forward placements, and options contracts, repurchase agreements, and securities lending arrangements, use them in a manner considered acceptable for use in a national bank's own investment portfolio.

    d. Ascertain whether investment companies whose shares are owned by the bank are registered with the Securities and Exchange Commission for public trading or are privately offered funds sponsored by an affiliated commercial bank.

    e. Determine if investment company shares are revalued quarterly and accurately reported.

22. On the basis of pricings, ratings, and credit analyses performed above, and using the investments selected in step 8 or from lists previously obtained, test for compliance with applicable laws, rulings, and regulations by:

    a. Determining if the bank holds Type II or III investments that have predominantly speculative characteristics or securities that are not readily marketable (12 CFR 1.3(b)).

    b. Reviewing the recap of investment securities by legal types, as defined by 12 CFR 1, on the basis of the legal restrictions of 12 USC 24, specific OCC Interpretive Rulings and competent legal opinions, as follows:

- If a Type II or III security is readily marketable, and if the purchaser's judgment was based on evidence of the obligor's ability to perform, determine if the par value of such securities issued by a single obligor, which the bank owns or is committed to purchase, exceeds 10 percent of the bank's capital funds (12 CFR 1.5(b) and 1.7(b)).
- If the holding of a Type II or III security was based on a reliable estimate of the obligor's ability to perform, determine if the aggregate par value of such issues exceeds 5 percent of the bank's capital funds (12 CFR 1.5(b) and 1.7(b)).

c. For those investment securities that are convertible into stock or which have stock purchase warrants attached:

- Determining if the book value has been written down to an amount that represents the investment value of the security, independent of the conversion or warrant provision (12 CFR 1.10).
- Determining if the par values of other securities that have been ruled eligible for purchase, are within specified capital limitations.

d. Reviewing pledge agreements and secured liabilities and determining that:

- Proper custodial procedures have been followed.
- Eligible securities are pledged.
- Securities pledged are sufficient to secure the liability that requires securing.
- Treasury Tax and Loan Remittance Option and Note Option are properly secured.
- Private deposits are not being secured.

(Information needed to perform the above steps will be contained in the pledge agreement; Treasury circulars 92 and 176, as amended; 12 USC 265; 31 CFR 203.15; 12 CFR 9.10; 12 CFR 7.7410 and 7.7415; and appropriate state statutes.)

e. Reviewing accounting procedures to determine that:

- Investment premiums are being extinguished by maturity or call dates (12 CFR 18 and 12 CFR 1.11).
- Premium amortization is charged to operating income (12 CFR 1.11 and 18).
- Lump sum write-offs of bond premiums are reflected as other operating expenses (12 CFR 18).
- Accretion of bond discount requires a concurrent accrual of deferred income tax payable (12 CFR 7.7505).
- Accretion of investment discount that totals 5 percent or more of annual investment income is the subject of appropriate notation for financial statement reporting purposes (12 CFR 18).
- Securities gains or losses are reported net of applicable taxes, and net gains or losses are reflected in the period in which they are realized (12 CFR 18).

f. Determining if securities purchased under agreement to resell are in fact securities (not loans), are eligible for investment by the bank and are within prescribed limits (12 USC 24, 12 CFR 1, and 12 CFR 7.1131). If not, determine whether the transaction is within the limits of 12 USC 84.

g. Reviewing securities sold under agreement to repurchase and determining if they are, in fact, securities and not guaranteed loans.

h. Determining that securities and money market investments held by foreign branches comply with 12 CFR 211.3 (Foreign Branches of Member Banks — Regulation K) as to:

- Acquiring and holding securities (12 CFR 211.3(b)(3)).
- Underwriting, distributing, buying, and selling obligations of the national government of the country in which the branch is located (12 CFR 211.3(b)(4)).

(Further considerations relating to the above are contained in other sections of 12 CFR 211. Also, review any applicable sections of 12 CFR 220 (Credit by Brokers and Dealers), 12 CFR 224 (Rules Governing Borrowers Who Obtain

Credit), Federal Reserve System Interpretations 6150 (Treating international bank securities as "exempted" securities under 15 USC 78c(a)(12)), and 6200 (Covering borrowing by a domestic broker from a foreign broker). Edge Act and Agreement corporations are discussed in the "Related Organizations" section).

23. Test for compliance with other laws, rulings, and regulations as follows:

   a. Review lists of affiliate relationships and lists of directors and principal officers and their interests, and:

      • Determine if the bank is an affiliate of a firm that is engaged primarily in underwriting or selling securities (12 USC 377).
      • Determine if directors or officers are engaged in or employed by firms that are engaged in similar activities (12 USC 78, 377 and 378). It is an acceptable practice for bank officers to act as directors of securities companies not doing business in the U.S., the stock of which is owned by the bank as authorized by the board of directors of the Federal Reserve.)
      • Review the list of federal funds sold, securities purchased under agreements to resell, interest bearing time deposits and commercial paper, and determine if the bank is investing in money market instruments of affiliated banks or firms (12 USC 371(c), and 12 CFR 7.7376 and 7.7370).
      • Determine if transactions involving affiliates, insiders, or their interests have terms that are less favorable to the bank than transactions involving unrelated parties (12 USC 371(c) and 375).

   b. Review sales receipts to determine if bank-owned securities or money market instruments have been purchased with funds held by the bank in a fiduciary capacity (12 CFR 9.12).

   c. Forward copy of the list of due from commercial banks or other depository institutions — time to examiner assigned "Due From Banks" to determine compliance with 12 USC 463.

   d. Determine if Federal Reserve stock equals 3 percent of the subject bank's booked capital and surplus accounts (12 USC 282).

   e. Review the nature and duration of federal funds sales to determine if term federal funds are being sold in an amount exceeding the limit imposed by 12 USC 84.

f. If the bank effects securities transactions for customers, determine if it is in compliance with 12 CFR 12 by substantiating Internal Control questions 37 through 48.

24. With regard to potential unsafe and unsound investment practices and possible violations of 15 USC 78j, review the list of securities purchased and/or sold since the last examination, and:

a. Determine if the bank engages one securities dealer or salesperson for virtually all transactions. If so:

- Evaluate the reasonableness of the relationship on the basis of financial condition, past securities enforcement actions, board approval, dealer's location and reputation.
- Compare purchase and sale prices to independently established market prices as of trade dates, if appropriate.

b. Determine if investment account securities have been purchased from the bank's own trading department. If so:

- Independently establish the market price as of trade date.
- Review trading account purchase and sale confirmations, and determine if the security was transferred to the investment portfolio at market price.

c. Determine if the volume of trading activity in the investment portfolio appears unwarranted. If so:

- Review investment account daily ledgers and transaction invoices to determine if sales were matched by a like amount of purchases.
- Determine whether the bank is financing a dealer's inventory.
- Compare purchase and sale prices with independently established market prices as of trade dates, if appropriate. The carrying value should be determined by the market value of the securities as of the trade date.
- Cross-reference descriptive details on investment ledgers and purchase confirmations to the actual bonds or safekeeping receipts

to determine if the bonds delivered are those purchased.
- Review and make a determination about trading activity taking place in the investment portfolio.
  - Review the FFIEC objectionable investment portfolio practices (BC-228), and determine whether these practices are taking place in the bank's investment portfolio.
  - Review recurring month-end securities purchases and subsequent resale at the beginning of the next month. Determine whether the bank is financing a dealer's inventory position or engaged in a practice of unwritten or verbal repos or loans to the dealer to carry inventory.

25. Discuss with appropriate officer(s) and prepare report comments on:

a. Defaulted issues.

b. Speculative issues.

c. Incomplete credit information.

d. Absence of legal opinions.

e. Significant changes in maturity scheduling.

f. Shifts in the rated quality of holdings.

g. Concentrations.

h. Unbalanced earnings and risk considerations.

i. Unsafe and unsound investment practices.

j. Apparent violations of laws, rulings, and regulations and the potential personal liability of the directorate.

k. Significant variances from peer group statistics.

l. Market value depreciation, if significant.

m. Weaknesses in supervision.

       n. Policy deficiencies.

26.   Reach a conclusion regarding the quality of department management. Communicate your conclusion to the examiner assigned "Management Appraisal" and the examiner-in-charge of the international examination, if applicable.

27.   Prepare a memorandum, and update work programs with any information that will facilitate future examination. If the bank has overseas branches, indicate those securities requiring review during the next overseas examination and the reasons for the review.

Review the bank's internal controls, policies, practices, and procedures regarding purchases, sales, and servicing of the investment portfolio. The bank's system should be documented in a complete, concise manner and should include, where appropriate, narrative descriptions, flowcharts, copies of forms used, and other pertinent information. Items marked with asterisks require substantiation by observation or testing.

Investment Securities Policies

1. Has the board of directors, consistent with its duties and responsibilities, adopted written investment securities policies, including WI securities, futures, and forward placement contracts, that outline:

   a. Objectives?

   b. Permissible types of investments?

   c. Diversification guidelines, to prevent undue concentration?

   d. Maturity schedules?

   e. Limitation on quality ratings?

   f. Policies regarding exceptions to standard policy?

   g. Valuation procedures and frequency?

2. Are investment policies reviewed at least annually by the board to determine if they are compatible with changing market conditions?

3. Have policies been established for transferring securities from the trading account to the investment securities account?

4. Have limitations been imposed on the investment authority of officers?

5. Do security transactions require dual authorization? *

6. If the bank has due from commercial banks or other depository institutions — time, federal funds sold, commercial paper, securities purchased under agreements to resell or any other money market type of investment:

   a. Is purchase or sale authority clearly defined?

   b. Are purchases or sales reported to the board of directors or its investment committee?

   c. Are maximums established for the amount of each type of asset?

   d. Are maximums established for the amount of each type of asset that may be purchased from or sold to any one bank?

   e. Do money market investment policies outline acceptable maturities?

   f. Have credit standards and review procedures been established?

7. If the bank holds shares of mutual funds or unit investment trusts, has the board of directors adopted policies and procedures that include:

   a. Specific provisions for purchases of mutual fund and unit investment trust shares?

   b. Requirements for prior approval of initial investment in investment companies?

   c. Procedures, standards, and controls for managing such investments?

Custody of Securities

8. Do procedures preclude the custodian of bank securities from: *

   a. Having sole physical access to securities?

   b. Preparing release documents without the approval of authorized persons?

   c. Preparing release documents not subsequently examined or tested by a second custodian?

   d. Performing more than one of the following transactions: (1) execution of trades, (2) receipt or delivery of securities, (3) receipt and disbursement of proceeds?

9. Are securities physically safeguarded to prevent loss or unauthorized removal or use? *

10. Are securities, other than bearer securities, held only in the name of the bank?

11. When a negotiable certificate of deposit is acquired, is the certificate safeguarded in the same manner as any other negotiable investment instrument?

Investment Securities Records

12. Do subsidiary records of investment securities show all pertinent data describing the security, its location, pledged or unpledged status, premium amortization, discount accretion, and interest earned, collected, and accrued?

13. Is the preparation and posting of subsidiary records performed or reviewed by persons who do not also have sole custody of securities? *

14. Are subsidiary records reconciled, at least monthly, to the appropriate general ledger accounts, and are reconciling items investigated by persons who do not also have sole custody of securities? *

15. For international division investments, are entries for U.S. dollar carrying values of foreign currency denominated securities rechecked at inception by a second person?

Purchases, Sales, and Redemptions

16. Is the preparation and posting of security and open contractual commitments purchase, sale, and redemption records performed or

reviewed by persons who do not also have sole custody of securities or authorization to execute trades? *

17. Are supporting documents, such as brokers' confirmations and account statements for recorded purchases and sales checked or reviewed subsequently by persons who do not also have sole custody of securities or authorization to execute trades? *

18. Are purchase confirmations compared to delivered securities or safekeeping receipts to determine if the securities delivered are the securities purchased? *

Futures Contracts, Forward Placement Controls

19. Do futures and forward contract policies:

    a. Outline specific strategies?

    b. Relate permissible strategies to other banking activities?

20. Are the formalized procedures used by the trader:

    a. Documented in a manual?

    b. Approved by the board or an appropriate board committee?

21. Are the bank's futures commission merchant(s) and/or forward brokers:

    a. Notified in writing to trade with only those persons authorized as traders?

    b. Notified in writing of revocation of trading authority?

22. Has the bank established futures and forward trading limits:

    a. For individual traders?

    b. For total outstanding contracts?

c. Which are endorsed by the board or an appropriate board committee?

d. The basis of which is fully explained?

23. Does the bank obtain prior written approval detailing amount of, duration, and reason:

a. For deviations from individual limits?

b. For deviations from gross trading limits?

24. Are these exceptions subsequently submitted to the board or an appropriate board committee for ratification?

25. Does the trader prepare a pre-numbered trade ticket?

26. Does the trade ticket contain all of the following information:

a. Trade date.

b. Purchase or sale.

c. Contract description.

d. Quantity.

e. Price.

f. Reason for trade.

g. Reference to the position being matched (immediate or future cash settlement).

h. Signature of trader.

27. Are the accounting records maintained and controlled by persons who cannot initiate trades?

28. Are accounting procedures documented in a procedures manual?

29. Are all incoming trade confirmations:

   a. Received by someone independent of the trading and recordkeeping functions?

   b. Verified to the trade tickets by this independent party?

30. Does the bank maintain general ledger control accounts disclosing, at a minimum:

   a. Futures or forwards contracts memoranda accounts?

   b. Deferred gains or losses?

   c. Margin deposits?

31. Are futures and forward contracts activities:

   a. Supported by detailed subsidiary records?

   b. Agreed daily to general ledger controls by someone who is not authorized to prepare general ledger entries?

32. Do periodic statements received from futures commission merchants reflect:

   a. Trading activity for the period?

   b. Open positions at the end of the period?

   c. Market value of open positions?

   d. Unrealized gains and losses?

   e. Cash balances in accounts?

33. Are all of these periodic statements:

   a. Received by someone independent of both the trading and

recordkeeping functions?

   b. Reconciled to all of the bank's accounting records?

34.   Are the market prices reflected on the statements:

   a. Verified with listed prices from a published source?

   b. Used to recompute gains and losses?

35.   Are daily reports of unusual increases in trading activity reviewed by senior management?

36.   Are weekly reports prepared for an appropriate board committee which reflect:

   a. All trading activity for the week?

   b. Open positions at the end of the week?

   c. Market value of open positions?

   d. Unrealized gains and losses?

   e. Total trading limits outstanding for the bank?

   f. Total trading limits for each authorized trader?

37.   Is the futures and forwards contracts portfolio revalued on a monthly basis to market value or to the lower of cost or market?

38.   Are revaluation prices provided by persons or sources totally independent of the trading function?

Recordkeeping and Confirmation Requirements for Customer Securities Transactions (12 CFR 12)

39.   Are chronological records of original entry containing an itemized daily record of all purchases and sales of securities maintained? (12 CFR 12.3)

40. Do the original entry records reflect:

   a. The account or customer for which each such transaction was effected?

   b. The description of the securities?

   c. The unit and aggregate purchase or sale price (if any)?

   d. The trade date?

   e. The name or other designation of the broker/dealer or other person from whom purchased or to whom sold?

If the bank has had an average of 200 or more securities transactions per year for customers over the prior three- calendar-year period, exclusive of transactions in U.S. government and federal agency obligations, answer questions 41, 42 and 43.

41. Does the bank maintain account records for each customer which reflect:

   a. All purchases and sales of securities?

   b. All receipts and deliveries of securities?

   c. All receipts and disbursements of cash for transactions in securities for such account?

   d. All other debits and credits pertaining to transactions in securities?

42. Does the bank maintain a separate memorandum (order ticket) of each order to purchase or sell securities (whether executed or canceled) which includes:

   a. The account(s) for which the transaction was effected?

   b. Whether the transaction was a market order, limit order, or subject to special instructions?

c. The time the order was received by the trader or other bank employee responsible for affecting the transaction?

d. The time the order was placed with the broker/dealer, or if there was no broker/dealer, the time the order was executed or canceled?

e. The price at which the order was executed?

f. The broker/dealer used?

43. Does the bank maintain a record of all broker/dealers selected by the bank to effect securities transactions and the amount of commissions paid or allocated to each such broker during the calendar year?

44. Does the bank, subsequent to effecting a securities transaction for a customer, mail or otherwise furnish to such customer either a copy of the confirmation of a broker/dealer relating to the securities transaction or a written trade confirmation prepared by the bank?

45. If customer notification is provided by furnishing the customer with a copy of the confirmation of a broker/dealer relating to the transaction, and if the bank is to receive remuneration from the customer or any other source in connection with the transaction, and the remuneration is not determined pursuant to a written agreement between the bank and the customer, does the bank also provide a statement of the source and amount of any remuneration to be received?

46. If customer notification is provided by furnishing the customer with a trade confirmation prepared by the bank, does the confirmation disclose:

a. The name of the bank?

b. The name of the customer?

c. Whether the bank is acting as agent for such customer, as principal for its own account, or in any other capacity?

d. The date of execution and a statement that the time of execution will be furnished within a reasonable time upon written request of such customer?

e. The identity, price, and number of shares or units (or principal amount in the case of debt securities) of such securities purchased or sold by such customer?

47. For transactions which the bank effects in the capacity of agent, does the bank, in addition to the above, disclose:

a. The amount of any remuneration received or to be received, directly or indirectly, by any broker/dealer from such customer in connection with the transaction?

b. The amount of any remuneration received or to be received by the bank from the customer and the source and amount of any other remuneration to be received by the bank in connection with the transaction, unless remuneration is determined pursuant to a written agreement between the bank and the customer?

c. The name of the broker/dealer used; or where there is no broker/dealer, the name of the person from whom the security was purchased or to whom it was sold, or the fact that such information will be furnished within a reasonable time upon written request?

48. Does the bank maintain the above records and evidence of proper notification for a period of at least three years?

49. Does the bank furnish the written notification described above within five business days from the date of the transaction, or if a broker/dealer is used, within five business days from the receipt by the bank of the broker/dealer's confirmation (12 CFR 12.5)? If not, does the bank use one of the alternative procedures described in 12 CFR 12.5?

50. Unless specifically exempted in 12 CFR 12.7, does the bank have established written policies and procedures ensuring (12 CFR 12.6):

a. That bank officers and employees who make investment recommendations or decisions for the accounts of customers, who participate in the determination of such recommendations or decisions, or who, in connection with their duties, obtain information concerning which securities are being purchased or sold or recommended for such action, report to the bank, within 10 days after the end of the calendar quarter, all transactions in securities made by them or on their behalf, either at the bank or elsewhere in which they have a beneficial interest (subject to certain exemptions of 12 CFR 12.6(d))?

b. That in the above required report the bank officers and employees identify the securities purchased or sold and indicate the dates of the transactions and whether the transactions were purchases or sales?

c. The assignment of responsibility for supervision of all officers or employees who: (1) transmit orders to or place orders with broker/dealers, or (2) execute transactions in securities for customers?

d. The fair and equitable allocation of securities and prices to accounts when orders for the same security are received at approximately the same time and are placed for execution either individually or in combination?

e. Where applicable, and where permissible under local law, the crossing of buy and sell orders on a fair and equitable basis to the parties to the transaction?

Other

51. Does the board of directors receive regular reports on domestic and international division investment securities, which include:

- Valuations.
- Maturity distributions.
- Average yield.
- Reasons for holding and benefits received (international division and overseas holdings only).

52. Are purchases, exchanges, and sales of securities and open contractual commitments ratified by action of the board of directors or its investment committee and thereby made a matter of record in the minutes?

Conclusion

53. Is the foregoing information an adequate basis for evaluating internal control in that there are no significant additional internal auditing procedures, accounting controls, administrative controls, or other circumstances that impair any controls or mitigate any weaknesses indicated above (explain negative answers briefly, and indicate conclusions as to their effect on specific examination or verification procedures)?

54. Based on a composite evaluation, as evidenced by answers to the foregoing questions, internal control is considered _____ (good, medium, or bad).

Investment Securities
(Section 203)

Verification Procedures

1. Test the addition of the investment and money market holdings trial balances.

2. Test the reconciliations of the trial balances to the general ledger.

3. If investment or money market holdings are held in safekeeping at locations outside the bank, request the safekeeping agent to provide lists of securities held including name, description, par value, interest rate, due date, pledge status, and payment date of next coupon. (For international division securities, all requests and direct verification should be made in the name of the bank, on its letterhead, and returned to its audit department with a code designed to direct such information to the examiners.)

4. Using appropriate sampling techniques, select investment and money market holdings from the trial balances and:

   a. For investment and money market instruments held at the bank:

   - Examine and count the securities.
   - Compare details of certificates to trial balances.
   - If securities are pledged to secure the bank's liabilities, determine that they are properly segregated from other securities.
   - Determine if coupons are intact.
   - Investigate any discrepancies.

   b. For investment and money market instruments not held at the bank:

   - Compare trial balance details to safekeeping receipts and the safekeeping agent's confirmation list.
   - Determine that pledge status, if any, is properly noted on the safekeeping agent's confirmation list.
   - Investigate any discrepancies.

   c. For investment and money market holdings purchased since the last examination:

- Verify cost by examining invoices, broker's advices, or other independent sources.
- Determine that the securities were properly recorded in the general ledger.
- Determine that purchases were approved by the board of directors or its designated committee.
- For investment and money market holdings purchased at a premium or discount, test book value by:
  - Determining the bank's method of calculating and recording amortization of premiums and accretion of discounts.
  - Determining the gross amount of premium or discount at purchase date.
  - Determining the period to maturity or call date.
  - Calculating the amount of premium remaining to be amortized or discount remaining to be accreted.
  - Determining that book value is reflected properly in the general ledger.
  - Investigating any discrepancies.
  - Scanning previously tested amortization or accretion schedules for investment or money market holdings acquired prior to the last examination and investigating any significant departure from these schedules.

5. Test gains and losses on disposal of investment securities since the last examination by sampling investment sales records and:

   a. Determining sales price by examining invoices or brokers' advices.

   b. Checking computation of book value on settlement date.

   c. Calculating gain or loss and tracing the amount to its proper recording in the general ledger.

   d. Determining that the general ledger has been properly relieved of the investment, accrued interest, premium, discount, and other related accounts.

e. Determining that sales were approved by the board of directors or its designated committee.

6. Test accrued interest by:

a. Determining the bank's method of calculating and recording interest accruals.

b. Obtaining trial balance(s) of accrued interest, if maintained separately from trial balances of investment and money market holdings.

c. Testing the addition of the trial balance(s) and the reconciliation of the trial balance(s) to the general ledger.

d. Determining that interest accruals are not being made on defaulted issues.

e. Randomly selecting at least one of each type of the various investment and money market holdings selected as sample items in step 4 and:

   • Determining the interest rate and last interest payment date of coupons and money market instruments.
   • Calculating accrued interest and comparing it to the trial balance(s).

7. Obtain and prepare, for each kind of investment and money market holding, a schedule showing the accrued interest balance and the investment balance at the end of each quarter since the last examination, and:

a. Calculate the ratios of accrued interest to investment balance for each type and time period.

b. Investigate significant fluctuations and/or trends.

8. Obtain or prepare, for each kind of investment and money market holding, a schedule showing the monthly income amounts and the average monthly balance since the last examination, and:

(This step should be performed only if the examiner-in-charge determines that it is necessary as an extension of similar computations made in NBSS reports.)

    a. Calculate yield.

    b. Investigate significant fluctuations and/or trends.

9.   If the bank is engaged in financial futures, forward placement, or stand-by contracts:

- Reconcile outstanding contracts to general ledger memoranda accounts.
- Determine the current market value (gross and net) of outstanding contracts.
- Confirm the existence of contracts with broker(s) doing business with the bank.
- For a sample of transactions currently outstanding and closed out since the last examination:
  - Verify cost and profit and loss by examining broker's preliminary and final confirmations, margin calls and margin runs.
  - Trace a sample of settlement funds and profit and loss entries to determine if they were properly recorded.
  - Determine if there is a high correlation between the contracts and offset to the contracts.
- Test fee income received by the bank in connection with the sale of a stand-by contract.
- Evaluate the credit risk exposure associated with various customers and dealers.

www.ingramcontent.com/pod-product-compliance
Lightning Source LLC
Chambersburg PA
CBHW080515290526
45790CB00006B/2174